The Mun

Growing Up in Ballymun

The Mun

Growing Up in Ballymun

Lynn Connolly

Gill & Macmillan

Published by Gill & Macmillan Ltd
Hume Avenue, Park West, Dublin 12
with associated companies throughout the world
www.gillmacmillan.ie

© Lynn Connolly 2006
ISBN–13: 978 07171 4042 8
ISBN–10: 0 7171 4042 3

Type design: Make Communication
Typesetting and print origination: Carrigboy Typesetting Services, County Cork
Printed by ColourBooks Ltd, Dublin

This book is typeset in Linotype Minion and Neue Helvetica.

The paper used in this book comes from the wood pulp of managed forests. For every tree
felled, at least one tree is planted, thereby renewing natural resources.

A CIP catalogue record for this book is available from the British Library.

5 4 3 2 1

Contents

Chapter 1
The Early Years

Having memories of somewhere that no longer exists is a bit like watching dead actors walking and talking in old movies. You can see the actor right there in front of you, but you know he is long dead; just as I can see Sean MacDermott Tower in my head, even though I know it was demolished in March 2005. On the Internet, I watched the video of the tower block imploding with a tear in my eye. It was surprisingly heart-wrenching to watch such an important part of my life disappear in a cloud of dust and rubble while the assembled crowd of Ballymunners, past and present, whooped and cheered. Somebody close to the camera repeated 'holy shit' several times as the fifteen-storey block of flats imploded in five seconds. And I have no doubt that people with fond memories of that tower block also shed a few tears that day; I certainly cried when I watched it fall. Sean MacDermott Tower is no more, and soon every last concrete flat in Ballymun will have been wiped from the Dublin landscape. But in my head Ballymun, and the people I knew there, will live on to the end of my days.

And yet I was one of the ones who wanted out. My need to get my children away from Ballymun and what it was becoming in the early 1980s was my main reason for moving hundreds of miles away. I can't deny that I wanted to get away from the broken lifts that stank of urine and vomit, the garda car chases, the needles left in the stairwells, the glue sniffers in the press on the landing . . . I couldn't wait to leave; and regardless of what U2 say in their song, 'Running to Stand Still', there was *certainly* more than one way out. And yet again, once I got out . . . I only ever hankered to go back. Because what I discovered when I left was that I had not only left Ballymun and its spiralling problems, I had also left behind some of the finest people it has ever been my privilege to call my friends.

Ballymun, as it was initially built, will soon no longer exist anywhere but in the memories of the tens of thousands of people who were born there and who lived and loved there. The 2,820 concrete flats are being demolished in a gradual 'regeneration' of the estate that will live on in the memories, both good and bad, of many people worldwide for some time to come. But within the time span of only a few generations all memory of Ballymun as it once was will be gone.

I hope that this time the planners have actually *thought* about what they are doing, because the original Ballymun, although unique and a place that provided cherished memories for so many people, was planning gone mad.

Built in the 1960s Ballymun was Dublin Corporation's knee-jerk reaction to the housing crisis of the time. Inner-city tenement slums like Summerhill and decaying suburban estates such as Keough Square desperately needed knocking down or modernising, and an expanding population in all areas of Dublin increased the need for housing to the extent that, by 1969, there was a waiting list for Corporation or Council housing of, on average, five years.

At the same time, it was next to impossible to get privately rented accommodation once you had children. Unless you could afford to buy your own house, you either lived with parents and in-laws, or rented whatever property you could get for what you could afford: in the late 1960s it could cost half a week's wages for the most meagre of rented accommodation.

Perhaps the idea of Ballymun would have worked better if inner-city communities had not been wrenched apart during the resettlement process. Would it really have been all that difficult for the powers that be to have re-housed people from well-rooted communities like Summerhill and Keough Square so that they still lived near to the families and friends that they had grown up with? Would it have made a difference? I can't answer that, because there is no way of knowing. All I know for sure is that when they put people into Ballymun they tore communities and families apart. But then, if that had not been done, the community that Ballymun became in its own right may never have happened.

Born in Yorkshire in 1956 to an Irish mother and an English father, I had lived a very average life up until 1966 when things started to change drastically in the mill town that I had known as my home. I had always been very aware of my Irish roots, and was, and still am, fiercely proud of my half-Irish status.

My maternal grandmother had given birth to my mother in the Dublin Union in 1926 after refusing to marry the man who had made her pregnant, then handed her child over to the dubious care of the nuns, refusing to give my mother up for adoption, for reasons that went with her to her grave. My grandmother then made her way to England, to Yorkshire, where she spent the rest of her days bringing up someone else's family. Of course it was only natural that my mother would eventually go looking for her own mother, which is how she ended up in Yorkshire, and how she eventually met and married my father. Had my grandmother married the man who had made her pregnant, or had she given my mother up for adoption I have no doubt that she (my mother) would have met and married an Irishman. But as things were, my mother had a desperate need to form a bond with her own mother, a bond that had been denied her all her life.

The other factor that prevented my birth happening in Dublin was the Irish social structure of the time. In 1926, even if she had desperately wanted to my grandmother could not possibly have brought my mother up alone. Her reasons for refusing to marry the man who had made her pregnant are as unclear as her reasons for not allowing my mother to be adopted into a normal family, but these choices were made nonetheless, and my mother was born, at a time when bringing a new life into the world was a shameful event for a woman without a wedding band on her finger. And like many a fatherless child of the time, my mother went to England, not only in search of a relationship with her mother, but also to get away from the draconian regime she had been brought up in.

Every August the mills would close and my parents would take me to Dublin for two weeks. I invariably came out in hives during the holiday, which my mother put down to the richness of the Irish food. We would visit relatives (people I have since discovered are not actually related to me at all), go to the zoo, the cinema, and all the other touristy things that people do on holiday. Then we would go home and normal life would resume.

My father had worked as a card minder at the same woollen mills for as long as I could remember, then suddenly, in early 1966, it closed down, and my father found it difficult to find another job. It was the same story all over England in the 1960s: unscrupulous employers were exploiting immigrant workers from Asia and the West Indies by paying them a pittance for long hours of labour. There was a time when it was possible to just walk out of one job and into another, but by 1966 jobs were being snapped up by immigrants who were prepared to work for a fraction of what my father needed to keep his small family. Life became a financial struggle for my parents, and so when he was offered a job in Dublin my father decided to jump at the chance of a decent standard of living.

However, the plan had its flaws. My parents had assumed that we would be eligible for council housing, just as we had been in Yorkshire, and it was only when we arrived in Dublin they discovered they would have a three-year wait at the least. We had arranged to stay with friends at first, and initially my parents were not perturbed by the fact that a council house was not in the offing. This simply meant that they would have to rent privately. But, as many people will remember, obtaining privately rented accommodation in Dublin at a time when the housing lists were full of desperate families was next to impossible. And so, when my parents found a caravan to let they jumped at the 'temporary' accommodation. I was only ten years old, so the prospect of living in a caravan was quite an adventure for me. Children don't see hardship in the same way that adults do; and I adapted quickly to a situation that made my mother cry herself to sleep night after night.

To call the area of grass at the turnoff to Ballymount from the Naas Road a 'caravan site' would be exaggerating a tad. A whole bunch of caravans parked up on the side of the road hardly constitutes what would be seen as a caravan site today. These days the necessities of life such as running water and sanitation would be a requirement of law. But in the 1960s the authorities didn't seem to give a damn that families with small children were living in such squalid conditions.

At any one time there were up to thirty caravans on the 'site'; full of families who were so desperate for somewhere to live that they put up with the difficult conditions just to keep a roof over their heads. Difficult? Perhaps 'harsh' would be a better word for the environment we lived in for the next three years. Everything my parents had been used to was gone. There was no electricity, therefore no television, no washing machine, no fridge and no electric lighting. Television was replaced by a radio that ran on batteries, my mother took the washing to a launderette once a week, in the summer milk would go sour overnight, and delicate gas mantles provided the lighting by which I read endless books.

Our chemical toilet was in a Little-House-on-the-Prairie type shed, just outside the caravan. But for many of the families residing there, the toilet was a bucket without the privacy of our little outhouse. There was only one place to get water: across the Naas Road, along the pathway and down a lane, to an abandoned farm with a standpipe in the yard.

The door of our caravan opened onto a panoramic view of the tip, the boundary fence of which was only a few feet from our home. This tip is now home to the Red Cow Hotel. The fancy hostelry that the Red Cow is now is a world away from what it was in the late 1960s, and the only cabaret was a singsong in the corner on a Friday night. Back then the Red Cow was a spit-'n'-sawdust kind of place where they sold the finest boiled ham I have ever tasted and the site around the Red Cow Hotel was home to the thousands of rats who lived on the waste products of society.

And Ballymun, well, Ballymun was a world with running hot water, flush toilets and central heating. I had heard of the fabled housing estate, but had never actually seen so much as a picture of it until my family was allocated a two-bedroomed flat in Sean MacDermott Tower in the early days of 1970. Having just come through yet another severe winter in the caravan, the prospect of such luxury was like winning the lottery.

Sean MacDermott Tower was one of seven fifteen-storey blocks that dominated the Dublin skyline. Each block was named after the seven signatories of the 1916 Proclamation of Independence. The other towers were Thomas MacDonagh, Eamonn Ceannt, Patrick Pearse, Oliver Plunkett, Thomas Clarke, and, last but not least, James Connolly. There were ninety flats to each tower, six to a floor. The other 2,190 flats, built in snaking rows around the coveted houses on the ground, were: Shangan Road, Shangan Avenue, Coultry Road, Balcurris Road, Balbutcher Road, Balbutcher Lane, Sillogue Road, Sillogue Avenue and Sandyhill Avenue. The 'roads' were all seven storeys high, and the 'avenues' four storeys. (The four-storey flats had no lifts, and getting home always entailed a trek up the stairs, ten flights when you lived on the top floor, no easy task when you had to cart the shopping, the kids and the pram up those stairs.) Massive expanses of grass between the flats and the houses, where children could run around and play, somehow managed to soften the concrete jungle that Ballymun was.

It may not seem much now, these days everyone has central heating and hot water on tap, and who still lives without a flush toilet? But in the late 1960s many things were an absolute luxury to most people. The norm then was to get up in the morning and set the fire, which heated the water via a back-boiler. The alternatives to this were gas or electric fires and an electric immersion heater, which were very expensive to run. Anyone of my age will remember winter nights spent under the weight of many blankets, and often Dad's overcoat thrown on top. But in Ballymun one blanket was often too much. When I was a kid, Saturday night was bath night, but in Ballymun you could have a bath every hour on the hour if you felt like it.

When I was a child I would wake up on mid-winter mornings to windows covered in beautiful patterns of ice. Jack Frost would come in the night and cover the panes of glass in intricate webs of frost that came from his finger-tips, or so my parents told me. My eldest son is now in his thirties, but he only found out about Jack Frost a couple of years ago; simply because the subject never arose in Ballymun. Ballymun made Jack Frost redundant!

On the day we were to view our new home for the first time we caught our very first number 36 bus from Parnell Square, with Alfie at the wheel, and set out to see the flat that was to become mine and my parents' home for many years to come. For some reason the buses that ran to Ballymun were generally single-deckers. I had *heard* of Ballymun of course, but had never seen it before that day when we got off the bus at the roundabout and stood looking around us in amazement at the mammoth housing estate. Alfie had kindly directed us to the underpass that ran beneath the enormous roundabout (which has since been filled in and a road laid on top), and we set off to find Sean MacDermott Tower.

That was the first time I had ever been in a lift, and my heart pounded with a mixture of fear and excitement as it took us to the twelfth floor. Back then there was no graffiti on the pale grey lift walls, no vomit or urine on the tiled floor and you could see, because nobody had nicked the fluorescent tube lighting, as they would do in the future. (I tell you, it is scary when the doors close on the lift and you are travelling upwards in complete darkness.) At the rear of the lifts a pair of locked doors stood, three feet high, behind which was a space that I was told would accommodate coffins. Realistically, it was probably there to accommodate stretchers too, but it was the coffin thing that stuck in my head. One night, when I was about sixteen, I had taken the lift and half-way to the twelfth floor a hand, swathed in dirty bandages, appeared out of this door. Did I stop the lift at the next floor and leg it? No, I grabbed the arm attached to the hand and pulled the little gurrier out of his hiding place. His pal only laughed when I put the little shit up against the wall of the lift by his throat and threatened to strangle the life out of him while he apologised over and over. Yes, he scared the shit out of me, but I reckon that feeling was mutual by the time I was finished with him. I suppose these days I would be done for assault for the same reaction.

I don't recall any coffins being taken out of the flats while I lived there, although I suppose there must have been *some*. (I know for sure that many coffins came out of the flats *after* we left Ballymun.) The flats were a transient place for most people, and so nobody really stayed long enough to die of old age. The dream of central heating and hot running water had become a reality; and so the dream of having a house on the ground became the next goal to achieve, and most did this within ten years or so. Of course, what they then found out was that central heating and hot water are very expensive to run in a house. Living in the flats meant that you paid a small amount each week, in with your rent, for constant hot water and heating. For a one-bedroom flat the cost was ten shillings and ten pence; if you had two bedrooms the charge went up to fourteen shillings and ten pence; with the highest cost being seventeen shillings and three pence (thruppence) for a three-bedroom flat. Nowhere in Dublin could you be so warm for such little cost.

Both the hot water and the heating were controlled from a large heating plant adjacent to Sean MacDermott Tower. This huge system pumped hot water through the labyrinth of pipes that ran between every floor of every block of flats. While this in itself was a colossal feat of engineering, it was not without its problems. When the system worked, everything was hunky dory; but when it failed, the warm, cosy flats became concrete boxes, offering little by way of comfort against the cold. Also, the heating was turned off from June to September, so any chilly summer nights could get very cold indeed sometimes. For safety reasons, gas was not piped into the flats, so most people had either electric fires or portable gas heaters as a back-up system. (Technically speaking, you were not allowed gas bottles in the flats, but everyone knew it happened anyway, electric fires being notoriously expensive to run.) The rent books stated that we were not allowed to keep any cows, pigs or chickens in the flat either, which was fine by us.

*   *   *

On our first visit to our new home we wandered round the huge, empty flat in wonder. Huge? After three years in a sixteen-foot, one-room caravan (with a heavy curtain in the middle that turned it into two rooms at night) this was a mansion in the sky to us. The flat was almost brand new.

The Corporation had provided cushion-floor lino, so there was no immediate need to worry about carpets. One of our new neighbours told us about the family that had lived there before us, and about how the father and daughter had moved when the wife died, apparently in the room that was to be my bedroom. But we didn't let this fact dampen our spirits as we bought furniture and moved into our new home.

The first few weeks were taken up with decorating and setting things right, nest-building if you like. Wallpaper was a doddle to put up in the Mun, you don't get many imperfect walls in prefabricated concrete, yet still my Dad managed to put the paper up crooked, but you couldn't tell from a distance. Mum had to have a 'china cabinet'. All mums seemed to have a china cabinet back then, where they would display all manner of interesting little objects alongside the best tea service and the 'good' glasses. They were usually bow fronted with etched glass doors, and took pride of place in living rooms all over Ballymun.

For my family, the move to Ballymun was about a lot more than central heating and hot water; to us it also meant electricity, something we had done without for the past three years. (In fact, running water in itself was quite a novelty. For the previous three years we had been carrying water containers across the very busy Naas Road several times a day, so we were even impressed with *cold* running water.) Of course, electricity also meant that television was now another dream come true. And not just RTÉ, like most people had in Dublin at that time. In Ballymun we had BBC and Ulster TV as well because another luxury that was provided for the people who lived on this new model estate was piped TV. There was a small charge for this, and a man came round the doors every week to collect it, but it was well worth the small payment to be able to see shows like *Top of the Pops*. My Mum got back in touch with the cast of *Coronation Street* and met the cast of *Crossroads* but never did quite get to grips with the new wave of TV shows like *Monty Python's Flying Circus* or *Rowan and Martin's Laugh In*.

My Dad heard that you could get HTV (Harlech Television) as well if you got an indoor aerial and pointed it in the direction of Wales. The big attraction for Dad was that HTV put on better movies than Ulster, and he would spend hours fiddling with a little rabbit-ears aerial trying to find the signal. His reasoning was that if people all over Dublin could get HTV via aerials on long poles, then so should he be able to bring the station in, being higher up that anyone else. He would walk up and down the balcony outside the flat with the aerial while Mum and me would say, 'that's better', 'worse', 'not too bad' and other such phrases, sighing intermittently. Then he got it into his head that the aluminium window-frame would be an aerial in itself and used all manner of Heath Robinson contraptions to secure the rabbit ears to the frame of the window. He would then have us sit in front of a snowy screen to watch some dreadful old movie or other, trying to convince himself and us that it was actually watchable. The Test Card was more watchable! One day he came home with a TV aerial that he could hardly fit in the lift. He tied it to the drainpipe out on the balcony, attached it to the TV and weyhey!—he *still* couldn't get HTV in any better. But I don't think he stopped trying until the day he left. He has Sky now, and is such a happy pensioner.

Back then, it wasn't only the piped TV man who came round the doors to collect money. So too did insurance men, loan companies and representatives of the parish church who called every Friday night for the 'collection'. Nobody was ever mugged. Nobody was scared.

Our new neighbours welcomed us, not least of all Bridie. Bridie was one of those women who always had the kettle or the chip pan on, always had a ready ear for anyone's problems, and gave alternatively sound and strange advice. (Bridie also made the most amazing cup of frothy coffee, long before the posh coffee houses came to Dublin. You put a spoonful of powdered, instant coffee into a cup with a spoonful of sugar. Add a teaspoonful of boiling water and stir like crazy until the coffee and sugar take on a pale colour, pour on boiling water and, hey presto, frothy coffee.) The trouble was that it was difficult to work out which of Bridie's recommendations was sound and which was strange, so you (well, I) did what she said anyway, just in case she was right. (She explained to us how each tenant took it in turns to wash the landing and sweep the stairs, and that didn't seem unreasonable.) Bridie lived with her husband and two children in a one-bedroom flat that looked out over the roundabout from her kitchen window. Many hours were spent sitting at her red, Formica-topped table under that kitchen window, drinking tea, taking advice and generally putting the world to rights, Bridie-style.

Poor Dad still worked over on the far side of the city, on the Long Mile Road in Walkinstown, and had to get four buses to and from work every day. But Mum and me were lucky, we got jobs in Quinnsworth, the biggest supermarket ever built in Ireland at the time, just across the road from Sean MacDermott Tower, in the brand new (not very imaginatively named) Seven Towers Shopping Centre. When it first opened people would come to Ballymun from all over Dublin to shop at the wondrous new superstore. Mum worked there as a cleaner at first, before progressing to the

canteen where, along with May O'Keefe and Lily Feighery
she fed the hundreds of staff who were ever grateful for their
stews, their pork chops and their braised steak, up until 1983,
when she retired. When I started, aged fourteen, I alternated
between stacking shelves, packing people's shopping, manning the gardening section and helping out in the coffee
bar (while all the time lusting for a check-out position).
2,820 flats, and some bright spark thought a gardening
section was applicable! No, we didn't do a lot of business. We
sold a few houseplants, but in general the idea was a flop.

I was sitting behind the counter of the gardening section
one day when I was startled out of my wits as the plate glass
door off to my right exploded onto the floor. The woman
who had just walked through the plate glass stood there in
shock with fragments of glass in her hair, but without so
much as a scratch to show for her 'accident'. The windows
and doors were so clean and shiny that she had thought it
was already open.

I would spend most of my time messing around with the
till while I waited for the occasional customer to buy the
occasional rubber plant—they really thrived in the heat of
the Ballymun flats. Except for the one my mother owned. I
used to shine the leaves with Mr Sheen—apparently that's
not very good for rubber plants—or bottle of Baby Bio. One
day I accidentally rang up £1,000 and the manager of the
store called me into the office and demanded to know where
the money was, obviously implying that I had stolen it. He
looked a touch red-faced when I pointed out to him that the
section was still fully stocked, and would have been empty
had I sold that amount of grow bags and rubber plants. The
same man was later sacked for going shopping at night-time
when the store was closed. Apparently, he would use his keys
to let himself into the store in the middle of the night and

then help himself to whatever he wanted. And he had the cheek to accuse me of being a thief!

I know that Quinnsworth and the shopping centre employed many security men over the years, but Mr McCullough is the one who sticks in everyone's mind: a great bear of a man, as hard as he was fair and as fair as the day was long. You could leave your pram, complete with baby inside, under his watchful eye, just inside the door of the supermarket, while you did your shopping. Local youngsters would run off with shopping trolleys and hide them in the underpass until they had a few together. Then they would take them back to Quinnsworth, telling Mr McCullough that they had been all over the place gathering them up for him, and he would give them 50p or a bag of sweets for their trouble. No doubt he knew exactly what they were up to, but he was a shrewd man who knew that friends were more important than enemies.

He died of a heart attack one day, in the storeroom at the back of the supermarket; my mother was there at the time and remembers it vividly. She said he very quietly walked into the back storeroom and into the little cubby-hole that he called his office before passing away. Mr McCullough was a one-off, and was missed by many when he left this mortal coil. So, while he may have allowed the kids to take the piss over the trolleys, those same kids felt sad when he died, and perhaps a little guilty. He could have played the hard man with them, but he chose not to, reserving those qualities for shoplifters. So when he died the local kids didn't say, 'Good riddance' but, 'Ah sure he was a nice man.' Tell me, how would you rather be remembered? Many a trolley boy will remember him as a hard taskmaster; but they will also remember him with a smile, and with respect for the good man that he was. God bless his soul.

Pat Quinn, what a lovely man he was; and just how many white, polo-neck sweaters did he own? He started to employ people a couple of weeks before the supermarket opened. But because everyone had to work a week in hand before they were paid, Pat Quinn gave everyone a week's wage at the end of their first week, in cash from his own pocket, so that they didn't have to wait a fortnight for their money. It was a gift, not a loan. He never intended for anyone to pay the money back. He was very much a hands-on kind of boss, and was a very visible presence in the store, as were the rest of his family. He was the most generous boss I have ever known, and he took care of his staff well.

He gave so many parties for us that I have probably forgotten most of them by now. I remember the night he paid for everyone to go to the Kiltiernan Sports Club. A very famous English impressionist (Mike Yarwood) was booked for the night's entertainment. Following a sumptuous meal we sat back and waited for the cabaret, only to be disappointed by a series of impressions of British politicians. Which were probably very good if you had the *vaguest* idea who he was impersonating. The very famous English impressionist was booed off stage, and the microphone was taken over by one of the young butchers who performed a stand-up routine to rival the best comedians. It was alternative comedy before the concept had ever been invented.

Quinnsworth provided a community where people not only worked together, but played together too. Perhaps Pat Quinn knew that this was the secret of a happy workforce. The free nights out didn't last forever, but someone would organise a knees-up every year, and coaches would take the staff to and from regular dinner-dances at places like the Portmarnock Country Club and the Green Isle Hotel, where you only ever had to pay for your drinks, without a care in the world about how drunk you got because the coach would be there to take you home at the end of the night, right to your block of flats. (I almost said 'right to your door', but that would have been exaggerating a tad.)

At every 'do' there would be raffles, spot prizes and those who could (as well as those who couldn't) would get up and sing a song or two with the obligatory live band. It seemed as though every live band in the 70s could play any song ever written. If they didn't know the song you wanted to sing they would say: 'You start, we'll follow you.' And inevitably they would do a grand job. Mrs Murray's rendition of 'Jerusalem' was awesome! And she performed it with gusto at every occasion, encouraging her captive audience to sing along with the few bits that they knew. My mother's party piece at these dos was 'McNamara's Band', as I am sure many local people will remember. It wasn't a do without a singsong, not in Dublin. (Which is probably why it took the Dublin people a lot longer than most to get along with the concept of discos. To Dublin people there was nothing like live music. Records had their place, and this was at home, where you couldn't really fit in a band all the time. In the late 60s and early 70s people went to discos, places like Zhivago's or The Star, but they still had live bands on. If there was no live music you felt cheated, especially if the drink was expensive too; you may as well have just stayed at home and played records, saving on the taxi fare home anyway.)

Quinnsworth took up an entire wing of the shopping centre that was the heart of the estate. Well, apart from the post office that had a little bit at the end. I remember the post office for the woman who ran it. Her name evades me, although I do remember that she was once shot during a raid on the post office, but she sticks in my memory as a nasty, bitter woman who really made me feel that she looked down on me. So much so that I used to dread going to the post office for anything, and would rather walk down to Glasnevin Avenue post office. The people who ran this post office were lovely, and had a cute little dog that used to jump over the counter to greet all the customers in the days before security screens. I wasn't the only one who would rather take the trek to Glasnevin Avenue rather than feel humiliated in the presence of the woman who never smiled.

Although there were some initial delays in the opening of the shopping centre, by 1970 every shop you could want or need was there, and the weekly trawl to the shops in town for the messages was eliminated. At either end of the shopping centre were two huge pubs, The Penthouse and The Towers. In between there were two butchers (Paddy's is the one I can remember the name of), two bakers (Johnston Mooney's and Mannings), grocers, betting offices, banks, a few clothes shops (last time I was there 5th Avenue was still selling ladies' and childrens' fashions), shoe shops and even hairdressers and barbers. There was a laundry and dry cleaners, and two banks, the Allied Irish and the Bank of Ireland. The latter was 'regenerated' some years later and went on to become Ballymun's own Labour Exchange. Up until then men still had to go into town, to Gardiner Street Labour Exchange, to sign on. But I suppose eventually the need for this facility outweighed the need for a bank.

Home Needs sold everything you could need by way of fabric and soft household goods, to the extent that business in that little shop generally resembled a busy market. They sold curtain and dress fabric, clothing, cushions, blankets, tea towels . . . if it was fabric based, Home Needs sold it.

They also used to run a 'club' whereby you could pay a little each week (usually for 20 weeks) to one of their agents, pick a number from a hat, and whichever week you picked you got to spend the full value of your weekly payments in one go. For example, when I ran an agency for that same shop everyone paid £2 for 20 weeks, giving each 'member' £40 to spend in one go on whatever week they pulled out of the hat. It was a bit disappointing to pull out the number corresponding to one of the last weeks, but by then you had committed yourself and couldn't pull out, and it gave you something to look forward to. In return for bringing in this extra custom Home Needs would give the agent the value of an extra week, so all in all it was not too bad a deal, and most people were members of the Home Needs club at some time or another. Over the years Home Needs must have supplied millions of yards of net curtaining: perhaps only passing pilots ever noticed, but in Ballymun people took great pride in their white net curtains. Two and a half times the width of the window was the standard size; that allowed for a good, full ruffle.

There were three shops where you could buy your daily newspaper; Jon's, Joe Wynn's or Miss Mary's. While Miss Mary's sold mostly newsagent items, with a few toys as a sideline, Jon's and Joe Wynn's sold just about everything they could fit into their little shops: sweets, ice-cream, groceries, cigarettes, toys, gifts, and they even had a deli section. Despite the presence of Quinnsworth, these small shops all did a roaring trade, mainly due to the fact that their owners worked all the hours God sent, including Sundays. (These days we are used to having 24-hour access to supermarkets, but in the early 1970s, late-night shopping was reserved for Fridays.) Although Jon's and Joe Wynn's were almost exactly the same in their stock loads and in layout, you were generally either a Jon's or a Joe Wynn's patron. Jon's is still there today, still selling the same range of goods that it did in the 1970s, although sadly it will soon be pulled down, like the rest of the shopping centre that stands all but deserted these days. The shops are still there, but the people are going elsewhere now. Quinnsworth became Crazy Prices and now: 'Sure Tesco's are ripping the people off, who can blame them for shopping at Lidl, at least there they get value for money,' one Ballymunner told me recently.

Back in the 1970s hardly anyone had a freezer, at least not beyond that of the ice-making compartment of the fridge. While a fridge was seen as a necessity for anyone living in the flats (the heat would curdle milk overnight and turn butter to oil), the balcony often had to do as a larder until you could afford one, but nobody had freezers, so shopping on a daily basis was indispensable. Joe Wynn's and Jon's would get in extra cooked meats for the weekend; not the pre-packaged, water filled, reconstituted rubbish that you get in little plastic boxes today, but great joints of beef, pork and ham that were put on the bacon slicer as and when a customer asked for it.

In the days before the EU got hold of the rules and regulations there was one slicer for all meats (and cheese), no gloves or tongs, and you only washed your hands when you went to the toilet. I can't remember anyone ever talking about the bacteria that could spread by handling food and money without gloves. But nobody ever seemed to get food poisoning, not that I know of anyway. The weekends also called for Joe Wynn's and Jon's to get in extra stocks of the blocks of ice-cream which were bought in furious fashion after every Sunday Mass along with the Sunday papers and the ham for the tea. Hundreds of people wearing their best Sunday clothes would descend on the two shops for their

Sunday World, cold meats and ice-cream; Neapolitan was always the most popular.

I worked at Jon's for a while in the early 70s. Jon and Jack, who were brothers-in-law, were great guys to work for. When I started there Jack explained that things sometimes got so busy that there wasn't the time to add things up on the one till, and he demonstrated how he added everything up in his head before putting the final amount into the till. He was awesome at mental arithmetic and to see him add up in this way was quite intimidating, but it wasn't long before I was pretty good at it myself, sums and mathematics being two completely different subjects. (Adding up prices is one thing; but when you start throwing in strange symbols and Greek bits; well, that's what mathematics is to me, or may as well be, Greek!) They (Jon and Jack) always appreciated their workforce and let them know it too. When it came to holiday time, I found a lot more money in my pay packet than I was entitled to. But when I pointed this out to Jack all he said was, 'Go have a good holiday, you deserve it.' I remember that you couldn't touch the till and the chiller cabinet at the back of the shop at the same time, otherwise an electric shock would be the result (a mild shock, but enough to make me squeal every time it happened). And great care had to be taken not to touch someone's arm while standing close together in that area, otherwise you would both feel the jolt at the same time.

There was a family of Travellers who would call into Jon's every week for their weekly shopping. They told me they didn't like supermarkets, and preferred the personal touch. Every week they would spend a fortune in the little shop on groceries that they could have got much cheaper in Quinnsworth. I have no idea where their money came from.

(There was a rumour that they would sign on in Dublin *and* in the North of Ireland every week, thereby getting double dole money. They certainly all seemed to drive British-registered cars around that time; so perhaps there was some truth in the rumour.) Every week the husband would pull out a roll of banknotes, remove the elastic band and pay for everything in cash. They were ever so polite, as were their children, the whole brood of them.

And then one week there was an extra child. The husband explained to me how his sister and her husband had been killed in a car crash in England and, because she had no other living relatives, the little girl (she would have been about twelve at the time) had been taken in by her family in Ireland; who were camped temporarily near Ballymun. Apparently the sister had gone to England fifteen years earlier, had met and married an English man, had her baby girl, and had settled into suburban life in London. This poor child had been brought up in a house, had gone to school, and had known nothing but romanticised tales of the ways of her Irish relatives until the alternative was for her to go into the care of local authorities. I cannot even begin to imagine what kind of culture shock that child must have suffered when she exchanged life in suburbia for life round a campfire. I never forgot her, and sometimes wonder what happened to her after that. But one thing I know for sure; that little girl was taken into the heart of a family that would love and protect her just like they did their own children.

*   *   *

The Penthouse and the Towers pubs both had an upstairs and downstairs section. Downstairs in both pubs there was a bar (men only) and a lounge, where women *were* allowed, and upstairs were cabaret lounges. (Actually, I don't think that the bars were 'men only' in any legal sense—in fact it was probably *against* the law to deny women access—it was more a case of the women preferring the comfort of the lounges to the more basic furnishings that were found in the bars.) The pubs also had off-licences, which were handy for when you ran out of fags late at night.

The huge pubs both did a roaring trade most nights of the week, and at the weekends the Penthouse was host to all of Dublin's top cabaret artists: Dickie Rock (women would shout, 'Spit on me, Dickie' at him at his shows, for some inexplicable reason); Sonny Knowles (There was a strange ritual attached to Sonny's appearances. Wherever he came on stage, women would stand up and reach out towards him with the palms of their hands, making window-washing gestures, which he would do back to them as he sang songs like 'A White Sports Coat'. Everyone said that Sonny should have made it to Vegas, but Sonny never wanted to be anywhere but Dublin, and the last I remember of him was in residency at the Drake Inn in Finglas.); Eithne Dunne; Colm Wilkinson, who went on to star in West End musicals; Joe Dolan (my lasting thoughts about Joe Dolan are how can any man sweat so much?); Eileen Reid (I still know every word to 'I Gave My Wedding Dress Away'); Mr Pussy (aka Alan Amsby—imagine a posh Lily Savage), and their resident cabaret singer Helen Jordan all performed to packed houses. The resident band was Vic Mellows and the Top Brass, and it seemed as though they could play every song that had ever been written. And if they didn't know it . . . well, they could follow you. Every weekend, Thursday to Sunday (including Sunday mornings) upstairs in the Penthouse was thronged with people who knew how to have a good time. And it wasn't only people from Ballymun who went to the Penthouse in the early 70s. People from Santry, Glasnevin etc, were happy to socialise with the people of Ballymun in the days before it all started to go wrong.

Sunday mornings at the Penthouse were stag mornings (not in the sense that anyone was getting married, just that no women were allowed) and Mr Gay and his jazz band played to exclusive male audiences. (I suppose he eventually had to change that name!) Nobody ever protested about these 'men only' mornings, which at the time were held in many pubs all over Dublin while the women stayed home and cooked the dinner. I only ever knew women to say, 'Sure why would I want to go and listen to jazz?' These stag mornings had nothing to do with strippers or lap dancers. Strippers were still strictly a Soho, London concept, and lap dancing hadn't even been invented (If 'invented' is the right word to use there. I mean, what's inventive about wiggling your bits in a guy's face?). Besides, no wife would have stood for that sort of behaviour in 1970s Ireland.

Not only did the Penthouse provide cabaret entertainment, the band played all night long, too, and there was a good-sized dance-floor to be taken up between cabaret acts. The entertainment manager thought up all manner of crazy ideas to bring in the punters. There always seemed to be a talent contest on the go, the first of which was won by Patsy Kavanagh singing 'The Big Grand Coolie Dam'. They made a record of him singing this song, but it never went on sale, it was only for Patsy. He was a lovely man, a gentle giant who used to go everywhere with his lumbering St Bernard dog beside him. They say that people and their dogs often take on a look of one another, and this was never truer than in the case of Patsy and his dog. (I'm not being unkind here, gravity takes its toll on everyone's face eventually.)

Patsy's wife Mary used to own a little two-seater sports car, with a soft top, which was forever being vandalised. So one night she took a long wire, attached it to a three pin plug, ran it down the side of the flats, attached it to the handle of the car and plugged it into the mains in her flat! Luckily for Mary the guards noticed the wire and put a stop to her handing out the death penalty for car theft. Although, in all fairness, I don't think she actually meant to kill anyone. She was always on the front line of any protest, even ending up in court on one occasion; the police had tried to move prams that mothers were using to block the dual carriageway, in protest at the water being turned off all the time, and Mary was having none of it. An exponent of Judo, she threw the gardaí back into their own squad cars before being arrested after a huge struggle. Mary, to the best of my recollection, was also one of the instigators of the rent strike of the 70s. When the Corporation wanted to put up the cost of the central heating for the flats, the rent strike was how the people of Ballymun reacted and for two years hardly anybody paid any rent. Eventually the Corporation had to bow to the pressure of the huge loss of revenue rather than to the solidarity of the people. But eviction notices were served on those tenants who had not kept their rent to one side for the past couple of years. But I digress; back to the Penthouse.

There would be drinking contests too, such as who could drink a pint the fastest, the twist being that it could be a pint of anything, from water to Guinness. (My mother won one of these contests once, drinking a pint of Guinness, in a record time that has never been broken. Vic Mellows said 'Start', then, 'We have a winner', without pausing for breath, as my Mum sank a pint of the black like her throat was a gaping hole.) Then there was who could drink a bottle of beer the fastest, through the teat of a baby's bottle. I don't know if you can still get hold of the old-fashioned style of teat that had to be stretched over the neck of a glass bottle, but it makes a cracking party game. All such fun nights were played to an appreciative audience and tasks were carried out to much cheering and loud encouragement from those watching. There was a contest called 'play that tune' whereby the band would be given the name of a published song and if they couldn't play it the customer got a prize, the condition being that the challengers had to be able to sing the unknown songs themselves. I only ever recall them being beaten twice, by a woman who knew the theme tune to *Scooby Doo* from start to finish, and by myself with 'Pokarekare Ana' (when I was eight years old I had a teacher from New Zealand who taught us the Maori song).

No food was on sale at the Penthouse other than crisps or nuts, so I suppose people must have got extremely drunk. Well you would *have* to be extremely drunk to go along with the nightly ritual on the dance floor. Just before the band played the National Anthem (in the days when everyone knew the words even if they weren't exactly sure what they meant beyond 'Soldiers are we . . .') they would strike up the theme tune to the TV show *Skippy the Bush Kangaroo*, and everyone on the floor would hop around doing kangaroo impressions. Grown men and women would hold up their hands like front paws, put on a buck-toothed expression and hop around like people in an out-take from *One Flew over the Cuckoo's Nest*. I know I am not the only one with this memory because Larry the barman still recalls the phenomenon with a chuckle. The band must have been wetting themselves laughing every night as they drove home to safe, secure suburbia.

One night there was plenty of room upstairs in the Penthouse. The Wolfe Tones were booked to appear, and the management thought it would be a good idea to put a poster up saying that there were hardly any tickets left; thinking they would all go in one rush. But people just thought, 'Ah, sure there won't be any left now', and so only a handful of people turned up that night. The oldest trick in the book; failed!

Once the Penthouse closed its doors at night the queues in the chipper (curiously called the Red Rooster when they sold more fish than chicken) reached epic proportions as the hassled counter staff tried to keep up with demand for smoked cod, plain cod, plaice or ray with chips. They also sold curry pies (beef and chicken), spice burgers, burgers in buns, roast chicken etc, and supplied vast quantities of food to the thronging, drunken masses that fell out of the Towers and the Penthouse every night of the week. It was also the place to get milk for the morning, but this was always a gamble: watching the supplies dwindle in the fridge as you made your way down the queue; would you have milk for the morning . . .? It was the worst feeling in the world when the person in front of you got the last pint and you knew you were going to have to make do with Marvel.

The chipper also sold groceries, although not cigarettes. They did a great line in broken and mashed chocolate as well, seconds from Rowntree's or Cadbury's. You could buy loose, broken Kit-Kat, and sometimes there would be no biscuit in them, so you would have the added bonus of paying knock-down prices for solid chocolate.

I was standing at the counter waiting to buy some broken Kit-Kat one night, when two boys came in. They were huddled together, giggling, and obviously were up to some mischief. They came up to the counter and stood next to me, hardly able to contain their excitement, as one of them placed a little brown mouse on top of the counter right in front of me. Now, if it had been a spider, or any sort of insect, I would have freaked. But a mouse . . . I like mice. I have never understood why anyone could be scared of such a cute little creature. So I picked it up and cuddled it in my hand, stroking its little head with one finger, much to the disappointment of the boys who had expected me to freak out. (One of the best things about living in Ballymun for me was that we hardly ever got insects in our flat, being so far off the ground that even the flies needed oxygen tanks to get to us.)

When Quinnsworth closed in the evening Joe Wynn's and Jon's would take over as the main shops, and when they closed there was the chipper, and when that shut, the garage near James Connolly Tower was open all hours. And of course there were the shop vans that were scattered around the estate.

It could be quite a walk to the shopping centre from Sandyhill Avenue when all you needed was a pint of milk and a batch loaf. When Ballymun was first built residents would take a short cut to the shops in Ballymun Avenue. But the residents of Glasnevin Avenue objected strongly to this and a wall was built (known locally as the Berlin Wall) to stop this access. And so the gap in the market was filled very nicely by the shop vans that began to appear all over the estate; but the Corpo hadn't thought about that. Did they really think that a mother of several small children would want to walk all the way from the end of Shangan Road to the shops just for a couple of items she may have forgotten, or run out of? No, I don't suppose they did; otherwise provisions would have been made for small shops in the basements of some of the flats during the planning stages. But then when it comes to The Mun, the planning departments never got out of the 'dream on' stage.

At first the shop vans really *were* vans that had been converted into static shops, but when the break-ins started the vans turned into shipping containers that were securely locked every night, yet your Ma would still say, 'Get us a pint of milk from the van.' And you never corrected her that it wasn't *actually* a van any more. Over time the vans became veritable fortresses to keep the thieves out. Shops that had once been caravans or buses were encased in steel right down to the ground (getting through a wooden floor in a caravan had proved no challenge to thieves with a power saw) and only a blowtorch would have got you into most of them without the keys. While these vans were dotted all over Ballymun eventually, the ones I remember being there the longest were Nelly's, at the bottom of James Connolly Tower, Tommy Doyle's, next to Sean MacDermott Tower and Tommy Watt's van which served the people of Sandyhill for many years, despite being broken into time and time again.

I remember a time, when two local gurriers broke into a particular shop van and took away a haul of cigarettes, chocolate and Fray Bentos steak and kidney pies. (I only recently found out that Fray Bentos is a port in South America.) The following day they went back to the same shop van, bold as you like, and sold the man back his own stock. Did he believe that they just *happened* to have the items he needed replacing, or did he know that he was buying back what had been nicked the night before? Perhaps he convinced himself that it couldn't be *his* stock because there were no tinned steak and kidney pies (the thieves in question had decided that the steak and kidney pies were just too difficult to part with). Or perhaps he *knew* it was his stock, but there was little point in trying to prove it, and it was probably the cheapest way of replacing what had been stolen. I suppose we will never know now. I apologise, but I can't help the gardaí with any ongoing investigation they may have in relation to this crime. I can't remember what year it was, I can't remember the names of the guys who did it, and even if I could . . .

You didn't have to go to the shops for *everything* you needed. In fact, if you waited long enough everything would probably come to your door. Carpets, lino, furniture, clothing, curious Louis XIV-style clocks with matching candlesticks, jewellery, electrical items, picture frames . . . If it was nickable (i.e. saleable), it came to the door eventually. Selling things in the flats was easy; you got the lift to the top floor and worked your way to the bottom via the stairs. (This method did not work too well in the case of the TV licence man. He would start at the top of the flats, and before he would be one floor down the word would have spread that he was on his way and hardly a door would be opened to him after that.) There was no such thing as a police patrol in the flats, so it was relatively safe to sell *anything* by this method. Nobody ever asked where the things came from; if you didn't ask, you didn't know, and therefore could not be troubled by your conscience in any way. Things came to your door in Ballymun, that's just how it was, and it never felt as though anything remotely unethical was going on.

A man knocked at my door one day selling family bibles on easy weekly terms. The Bible was/still is, very lovely, and as my parent's 25th wedding anniversary was approaching I decided to buy one as a gift for them. The man assured me that someone would call every week for the payments, and I didn't have to give him a deposit. The bible duly arrived in the post, but nobody ever came for the payments. I heard on the grapevine that the collector had been mugged, and so the company had decided to pull out of Ballymun. Did I contact the company to make alternative payment arrangements? No, I simply thought, 'free bible'.

Chapter 2
Single Parents and Poverty

The estate was full of young families with children. In the early 1970s the health centre was a row of dark brown, prefabricated buildings at the back of Sillogue Gardens, where the infamous Dr Byrne sat in residency as he dished out 'the Roche' (Valium) to women who believed him when he said it would help. This building was also where St James's hospital had their weekly ante-natal clinic, and it was always busy. Back then Ballymun was mainly inhabited by couples in their 20s and 30s, and so extensive procreation was the natural result.

However, in Dublin at that time (and I suppose in the rest of Ireland) there was no such thing as a 'single parent'. There were two official ways in which a woman could be on her own with children; she was either given the title, 'deserted wife' or, 'unmarried mother'. And Ballymun had more that its fair share of 'deserted wives'.

To clarify what I mean by this term: when a married couple split up in the late 60s/early 70s, for whatever reason, the woman stayed with the children, was classed as 'deserted' and could then claim welfare payments for herself and her offspring. But only once she had satisfied the relevant authorities that she had no idea where her husband was. (Which usually entailed lying to the authorities. If a 'deserted wife' knew where her husband was she was expected to get the money from *him* that she needed to live on. But a man on his own, even if he were in full-time employment, would have had a hard time coping financially with the high costs of private accommodation and living expenses for himself and for his family. So even when a wife did get 'a few bob' from her ex-husband, it was rarely enough to cover the cost of bringing up a family.) And then she had to satisfy the means test. A representative of the government would come out and tell women what they should sell in order to raise money. It was quickly pointed out that you couldn't be suffering *that* badly if you had a television, a washing machine or any jewellery beyond a wedding ring. Items that had taken years to get, TVs, washing machines, fridges etc, had to be sold and the money spent on food and household bills before the welfare people would believe that the family really were destitute. There was no such thing as divorce, and even if you went to England and obtained one, it was not recognised by the Irish authorities.

But there were no such welfare payments for unmarried mothers. Hence, there *were* no unmarried mothers. In fact, I wonder if I have the accolade of being the first in Ballymun?

If a girl got pregnant outside marriage it was the done thing to send her off to her Aunt in the Country (a common euphemism for St Patrick's on the Navan Road) and for the child to be quietly put up for adoption whether the girl in question agreed or not. Unless the girl's parents were prepared to help, there was nothing else they could do. You had to be married to apply for council or corporation housing, you needed to pay for child-care in order to work, and no private landlord would let a property to an unmarried mother anyway—even then it was way too big a scandal for any respectable landlord to deal with. Unless she wanted to live on the streets and beg for a living, there was no way an unmarried mother could even *think* of keeping her child without help from some quarter. When a girl found herself pregnant outside marriage in Ireland in the early 1970s she may as well have been in Dickensian London for all anyone cared.

Once a married woman had been classed as 'deserted' by her husband the only way for her to start a new relationship with another man was either by breaking the law or by living apart from the man she loved. (For a woman to claim Deserted Wives' Allowance while living with a man she was not married to was fraud, and fraud was a serious crime.) No matter why a married couple separated, even if the man beat his wife black and blue every night of the week, there was still no legal way of ending the marriage and starting a new life without flouting the law. There *was* such a thing as a legal separation. But this was meaningless. A legal separation was just that; a couple were separated legally. It didn't mean that either man or wife could marry again. Once a married woman started to claim 'deserted wives allowance' she could not have another man living with her under *any* circumstances without being accused of cohabitation by the welfare people. The only way that a couple could live together without being married, without breaking the law, was if the man had a good job and could take over the financial running of the household immediately on moving in. Of course, such men that were prepared to take on a woman and her children were rare. Living 'in sin' with a married woman was something that most Irish families simply would not have tolerated.

But people have feelings, something that Dublin Corporation and the welfare people never accounted for when they put their rule books together, and because people fell in love it was an inevitability that they were going to start living 'over the brush'. In the old communities, in the days before Ballymun was a twinkle in the eye of the head of the planning department, people got married and stayed together for life, whether they wanted to or not. The swinging sixties might have come to Dublin at the same time as it hit America and England, but attitudes to marriage were still very much in the Dark Ages. Generations of families used to live on the same streets in the same area, and perhaps that meant that young married women didn't have so much stress on them as the mothers who felt isolated in the flats in Ballymun. Not only that, but prior to the days of Ballymun you would go to your parents, or even to the priest with whatever troubles you were experiencing, and someone was always there to help you out with a bit of encouragement and wise advice. I am sure there must have been many couples who split up once they moved to The Mun simply from the frustration of feeling so isolated. Rows would break out, and without the buffer zone of the family to turn to, they had escalated into something more serious, and before you knew where you were another 'deserted wife' was picking up her allowance book.

For every 'deserted wife' there was a man who was alone too, and he was in the same impossible situation of not being able to start a new relationship unless he was prepared to live in sin. And if you're going to live in one sin, sure you may as well take on a few more. And so it came about that deserted wives claimed their allowance, while they lived with men who were claiming single men's dole. I know what you're thinking: why didn't the men just claim for the woman and the children? Because *that* wasn't allowed either. For a man to claim the dole for a woman and her children he *had* to be married to the mother, it was that simple. It wouldn't have mattered if the couple had lived together for years and had children together, their relationship would not be recognised by any of the relevant authorities. A family of four would have had problems living on single men's dole money without any form of alternative income, and so a deserted wife had no other option than to continue claiming the allowance that she was no longer entitled to once a man moved in with her.

It was an impossible situation for many, and there were no winners. There were no real financial gains to be had by claiming welfare payments separately, but it was illegal just the same, and if you were caught your allowance book would be taken from you. And it was at this point that many deserted wives discovered where and how to get all the freebies they could from whatever organisation they discovered.

All over Dublin there were religious organisations making sure that anyone in dire financial straits would have at least the basics of survival. The Society of St Vincent De Paul provided many a Ballymunner with the necessities of life: beds, blankets, shoes for the children etc, mostly to women who were left alone to bring up their children. And all over Dublin there were places where you could buy good quality second-hand clothing that nobody would recognise in Ballymun. The Ivy Market off Thomas Street was an out-and-out goldmine for clothes or household things, and all for pence. And on a Saturday morning at The Hill (famed by Lee Dunne) it was possible to pick up all sorts of bargains (my most memorable item being a black coat from Arnott's, which was perfect and purchased for less than a pound). In times of fiscal emergency, these wonderful places were a necessity of life. Pride didn't come into it; a mother did what she had to in order to provide for her children once she had been abandoned by her husband and the State.

It was quite rare for anyone to be caught out by the welfare people when they lived together illegally in The Mun. Unless you really pissed somebody off and they reported you, nobody ever really discussed the subject, it was simply a matter of course, a sign of the times, and a sign of things to come that people were not prepared to live alone for the rest of their lives. Some couples were married; some couples were not. And in the great big scheme of things, sure what did it matter? So long as the kids were taken care of. Anyway, once it was confessed to the priest . . .

There was a welfare office in the health centre, where you could apply for financial assistance at times of extra need, like when you needed help with First Holy Communion or Confirmation outfits. You would queue for hours, and then have to explain why you were so desperate that you were willing to go through this humiliating procedure to a pompous bureaucrat who never failed to see you off with a feeling of inadequacy. Even though they only gave the bare essentials, they managed to make you feel as though the money were coming out of their own pockets.

Once on welfare payments, though, you never had to eat margarine again. For some obscure reason the government felt it essential that everyone on welfare should have real butter on their bread. Butter vouchers were provided to every family with the weekly payout, which could be exchanged in any shop for best Irish butter; and in some shops for anything else you might need like Neapolitan ice-cream on a Sunday. You may have been poor, but there was always plenty of butter for your bread or your potatoes.

Small babies in families on low incomes were provided with powdered milk and baby rice in the same way, and all families on low incomes qualified for a medical card, which authorised free medical and dental treatment and free prescriptions. The medical card system was used to its fullest by many people who not only got medicine but also shampoo, cotton wool, nit treatment and anything else they could think of, while the going was good. There are those who would say that some people abused the medical card system; but I call it utilising the resources available. When you are on a very limited income and someone tells you that you can get so much more than you ever thought on a prescription, well, it's off to the doctors you go with whatever story you need to tell in order to get what you need. Money saved on shampoo could go towards other, more essential items, like shoes for the kids' feet.

Technically, unmarried mothers did not exist in Ireland in the late 1960s/early 1970s, and so they were not allowed the luxury of butter vouchers (Although their babies *were* allowed the same vouchers for powdered milk and baby rice as any other child. I chose to feed my babies on Ostermilk, which my mother still calls Oystermilk.) because they had no eligibility to claim *any* allowances for themselves or their child. Unmarried Mothers' Allowance simply did not exist. The government buried their heads in the sand and completely ignored the needs of these desperate women. If you could prove that you had no income whatsoever, and that you and your child would die of hunger without it, there was a small payment that could be claimed from the grubby little welfare offices which were dotted all over the city. But these payments were only to cover the basics, and did not allow for things such as utility bills or rent. If an unmarried mother managed to get some kind person to take her in rent free, then she could claim this meagre payment that just *might* keep her and her children in egg and chips for the week. It didn't even allow for essential items like clothing and toiletries, that's what the Society of St Vincent De Paul and the welfare office at the health centre were there for. The authorities put every block they could on the notion of unmarried mothers keeping their children. It was not a matter of choice! When I became pregnant outside marriage, in spite of living in a cosmopolitan city, I could not have coped without the full support of my parents and my employers.

Strangely enough, when I became an unmarried mother, people in Ballymun didn't seem to bat an eyelid. Unless I was so naive that I didn't notice them doing it behind my back, nobody ever looked shocked beyond the level of raised eyebrows when they found out I was going to have a child and that I was not married. Thinking about it now, I was probably the talk of the estate, but I was far too wrapped up in the impending birth of my child to notice if I was the subject of gossip. All I know for sure is that nobody in Ballymun showed me any form of open hostility. When Bridie first found out I was pregnant (told second only to my parents) she advised me to take a tablespoon of liquid paraffin every day, and my baby would be born with beautiful skin. So off I went to the chemist in the shopping centre and bought a bottle of the slimy, noxious, clear fluid. I took one tablespoon and nearly threw up before spitting it into the sink and deciding that my baby would just have to be born with crinkly, red skin like all other babies. But, so as not to have Bridie on my case, I tipped a tablespoonful of the foul stuff down the sink every day (I knew she would check to see that I was taking it). When my son was eventually born with a flawless complexion Bridie said, 'See, I told you the liquid paraffin would work.' And I just stayed quiet; until now. Sorry, Bridie, but liquid paraffin does not taste good!

When I told my parents that I wanted to keep my child they took it on their broad shoulders and supported me all the way and never once tried to get me to change my mind. There were only two occasions when I recall adoption being mentioned. The first time being when my mother heard about this wonderful place on the Navan Road where unmarried mothers could have their babies. Not that she wanted to hide me away from the neighbours (it was a bit too late for that), but that she had heard I could have my baby there in comfort, with other unfortunate girls who could relate to my situation.

She brought me there one Sunday afternoon when I was about six months pregnant. It was a big, dark, old convent, surrounded by high walls, a grey and foreboding building that would have made the ideal location for many a movie adaptation of Dickens' classics. A very austere nun—I always have been and always *will* be scared of nuns; but that's another story—took us into her office and, over tea and biscuits, explained how things worked at St Patrick's, before she showed us around. She took us on a guided tour of all the places that young, pregnant girls could scrub or polish floors and staircases. It was not difficult for Mum and me to understand for ourselves how St Patrick's worked, as the evidence of the hard labour pregnant girls had to endure was right there for us to see. The tour also took in the kitchens, where the smell of cooking cabbage was so strong that the same smell makes me feel sick to this day.

The nun then took us outside to show us the gardens; not nice lawned areas with rose bushes planted but vegetable gardens that provided food for the girls and the nuns. Once again pregnant girls were hard at work at all the tasks the nuns didn't seem to want to do. I can still see one girl now, wearing a huge grey dress and Wellington boots; she leaned on the fork she was using to turn over the soil and wiped the sweat from her forehead with the back of her hand in a scene reminiscent of a Catherine Cookson novel. All over the convent pregnant girls scrubbed, cleaned and polished with sweat dripping from their brows while the nuns . . . the nuns supervised and prayed. Slavery would not be too harsh a word for what I witnessed at St Patrick's; it certainly didn't resemble what I understand to be charity. Even now it seems to me that the girls were being punished, while the men responsible for getting them pregnant just carried on with their lives as normal.

I expected to be shown where my room would be should I decide to go there to have my baby; but instead I was shown a huge dormitory where all the pregnant girls slept together in one room until they give birth. It was like an enormous hospital ward, with tubular steel beds and individual lockers. Then we were shown the cubicles, which was really just another dormitory with thin panels between the beds, which the girls moved to once their babies were born. There were no doors, and only curtains were provided to give nursing mothers a little privacy as they breast-fed their babies. It was made perfectly clear that bottled milk was not acceptable, and it was the first time I had even *thought* about how I was going to feed my child.

The other thing that was made perfectly clear at St Patrick's was that every child born in that terrible, grim place would be put up for adoption at the end of six weeks. Now, how cruel is that? These girls were expected to give birth, breast-feed their babies, spend every day with them for six whole weeks, then just as the newborns were beginning to develop little personalities of their own, just as they were really starting to recognise their own mothers, the girls had to give them up for adoption. Love didn't seem to come into the equation at all. The fact that seemed to have utmost importance to the nuns was that the girl could then go home and resume a 'normal' life.

It was made very clear that having a child outside marriage was one of the most shameful of sins in the eyes of God; and yet it was a shame that the nuns were prepared to be party to. Is it right to cover up for another's shame when you really believe they have done something so very, very evil? They had no perception of the fact that no woman can live anything close to a 'normal' life when every day henceforth would be taken up with thoughts of the child that was wrenched from their arms.

The nuns really believed that they were providing a service for the girls in their 'care'. They could even arrange for my parents to receive regular mail from where I was supposed to be staying with my 'Aunt'. My mother thanked the nun for her time then took me home to Ballymun, and we never mentioned that place again. However, it obviously left a big imprint on my memory.

The only other time that adoption was mentioned was one day when I was in the lift with a woman who lived on the floor above. She was due her baby around the same time as me. She asked me if I would get to know who adopted my baby. When I told her I planned to keep it, she only said, 'Oh!' Stunned into silence by the fact that an unmarried mother intended to keep her child. Did she really believe that I could love my child any less than any other mother because I didn't have a gold ring and a pay packet? Probably. There were still many people in Ireland at that time who believed the shame of giving birth outside wedlock outweighed the prospect of giving up a child for adoption; that the shame could somehow be worse than the loss. Of course, the unmarried mothers knew different.

In the early 1970s there was no such thing as sex education in school. The closest schooling ever got to sex education was when the concept of 'original sin' as performed by Adam and Eve was discussed in catechism classes. And most kids hadn't got the faintest notion that 'original sin' was a euphemism for sexual activity. There wasn't much point in asking when you didn't really understand something; as we all know the stock-in-trade answer from the priests and the nuns on any subject they were uncomfortable with was, 'A Mystery'. I know that to me original sin was just the hugest sin ever. But the meaning behind the term had never been explained to me.

The closest anyone ever came to telling me the facts of life was when I was eleven years old and my mother told me: 'You might start to bleed soon. But don't worry about it, it just means you have become a woman.' However, she omitted to say from where, for how long, or any of the finer details that go along with the onset of menstruation. So for the next couple of months I watched women very carefully, looking for signs of this 'bleeding'. I was always curious when I saw a woman with a huge plaster. But I couldn't work out why a bleed on your forehead would turn you into a woman! A year is a long time at that age, and when my period finally did arrive I had completely forgotten about what my mother had told me. And I couldn't go running to her when it did happen because she was away, nursing my dying grandmother. Obviously, I was dying, too. Nobody ever bleeds that much and lives. But I was haemorrhaging from such an embarrassing area that I could not possibly tell my father.

But after a few days I got better, and wasn't going to die after all. Phew! So I carried on as normal, but of course a month later I got 'sick' again, and this time I was so sure that I was dying, it must have shown on my face. 'Whatever's the matter, pet?' my mother's friend asked as she saw me coming home from school one day wearing the longest 'I'm going to die' face in the world. I didn't need much encouragement to burst into tears, and she brought me inside. With a strong cup of tea in front of me I told her how I was dying. And when she finally stopped laughing she explained it all to me. Well, she said *something* anyway. 'It's only the curse. Sure we all have to go through it. What you have to remember now is that you mustn't let any boys touch you until you are married, or you could end up with a baby.'

I was cursed! A matter this woman seemed to find highly entertaining (or was it just my ignorance she was laughing at?). And if a boy touched me I could end up with a baby. What? If I touched a boy's arm he would put in an order to the stork? Confusion reigned in my little head, just as it must have in the heads of so many others at that time.

There must have been *some* liberal parents who told their children the facts of life, but in general most people picked it up as they went along. The trouble with this method of learning was that it was difficult to sift out the wrong from the right information. Like any other teenager I believed the crap that was being passed around verbally, and knew nothing of the biological workings of the human body. You can't get pregnant if you do it standing up; it's OK if you pull out on time—known as the CIE method; certain times of the month are safe. In Ireland in the early 70s there were no biological facts to back up any information passed along the grapevine. With such ignorance it was inevitable that girls had to visit an aunt in the country from time to time.

While I had yet to work out the details of how my own body worked I soon figured out that there were certain freebies that came along with pregnancy, so when I attended my first antenatal class at the prefabs in Sillogue Gardens I presumed that, when the nurse asked me for my shoe size while she was weighing me, I would be getting free shoes. Nobody explained that the size of my feet had anything to do with the proportions of my pelvis. In fact, I still don't understand how that one works.

Antenatal classes in the early 1970s consisted of a weigh-in, blood tests and having nurses and doctors put that infernal plastic cone on your belly to listen to the baby's heartbeat. Those things really hurt when they dug into your belly! Not at any stage of the proceedings was *anything* explained to me about how birth took place. Not that I needed it explained to me, because I had already managed to work it out for myself; as follows:

When the baby is due the mother goes into hospital. Once there she is put to sleep, her belly button is undone, the baby is taken out and the bellybutton is sewn up before the mother is gently woken from the anaesthetic to be handed her newborn child. How simple was my design compared to reality? However, because I assumed I was right, and everyone else assumed that as I was pregnant I must be aware of what was going to happen, the subject was never discussed (not even with Bridie). Who was it that wrote, 'To assume is to make an ass out of you and me (*ass-u-me*)'? Thomas Harris, I think.

Reality came to me during the showing of a film at the Plaza Cinerama on Parnell Square (now a waxworks museum). My friend Katherine had thought it would be a good idea for us both to find out exactly what happened when a woman gave birth, and I didn't need much coaxing, as I was pretty sure I knew most of it already. Every night there were queues round the block for the showing of a Scandinavian film called *Helga* to packed audiences, while representatives of the Legion of Mary protested outside at the 'pornographic' content of the film. The porn in question being: a woman giving birth. It can't have been a very good movie, because it's not available on Amazon, but there was full-frontal nudity; there may have been a baby coming out of that ten-foot-high fanny, but it was a *bare* fanny nonetheless, and people were turning out in their droves, queuing for hours to see it. It was 'standing room only' every night of the week. Such depravity in a country that had yet to allow women to appear topless in magazines and newspapers was sensationalism at its very best, and for me it was a very rude awakening to discover that babies came out the same way they went in. Let me tell you, that was a heady knowledge for me to have to take in when I was already six months pregnant.

On the way home on the bus after the viewing of *Helga* Katherine couldn't apologise enough. 'I'm so sorry,' she said, 'I had no idea that . . .' But she couldn't find the words to say what she had just seen. She still looked a little green around the gills when we got home to The Mun. However, it can't have really bothered her all that much, because she later went on to have at least five children. Katherine (which is her real name) was a good friend who stuck by me throughout my pregnancy when she could have been off out enjoying herself.

When I asked other mothers in Ballymun about their experience of giving birth they shrugged it off, like bringing a baby into the world was the easiest thing a woman ever had to do in her life; almost putting it across as a pleasant experience, something not to be missed. OK, slight exaggeration, but they all assured me that it was a pain you forgot all about once the birth was over, and anyway, it wasn't all that bad. So I settled for a level of 'not that bad' pain in my imagination, which was not even *close* to the real experience when the time came; one Thursday morning as I was doing my mother's hair.

To be fair on myself, I know I was far from being the only one to be pregnant with not much idea about how the baby was to be born. Some years later I came to know another woman who lived in Ballymun who had found herself in the same situation about a year after the birth of my first child. She and her friend, who were both in their 20s, were due their first babies around the same time, and neither woman had a clue as to what was going to take place. So they decided that whichever of them went into labour first would tell the other everything that happened in graphic detail. To save embarrassment to them both we will call my friend Mary, and *her* friend Ann.

Ann went into labour first, and when she came out of hospital a fortnight later she told Mary how the pain had been getting pretty bad when the doctor had given her an injection, and when she woke up again the baby was there in a cot beside her. She showed Mary the scar that ran from hip to hip to prove it. Ann told Mary that it was called 'a section' and Mary just assumed this to be another term for giving birth.

A couple of weeks later Mary went into labour and duly ended up in the labour suite at the Rotunda while her helpless husband paced the floor outside. Her pains were getting worse, and being alone didn't help. But there were no such concepts as 'birthing partners' back then, and men were completely banned from the labour suites. She called over a nurse.

'When will I be getting the injection?' she asked.

'Ah, sure, you don't need the pethadine just yet,' the nurse told her.

Presuming this to be what was to put her to sleep while the doctor took out her baby Mary asked, 'So when will you be putting me to sleep?'

'Now why would you want to go to sleep at the height of labour?' the nurse asked.

'So that you can take the baby out,' Mary replied, confident that she knew what she was talking about. The nurse frowned.

'Now why would we want to do that? We will need you wide awake to push baby out,' she explained, and Mary's head started to reel at the prospect of being cut open from hip to hip while she was still in her senses. She began to cry and babble incoherently at the nurse, trying to tell her that she would rather be asleep while she was cut open, and little by little the nurse realised that Mary thought all births were by the caesarean method. Mary went on to discover what natural childbirth was all about, and another five times after that!

I suppose how I discovered how babies are born was not too bad after all, not as bad as poor Mary and Ann anyway. But I have to wonder; there was Ann and Mary and me; all in the same boat, all three of us totally ignorant as to how babies were born. So how many more were there? How many of the girls who had their babies at St Patrick's and other such institutions had not got the slightest idea how they got pregnant in the first place? It seems almost unbelievable that as recently as thirty years ago, many women, even when they were married, were so uninformed about their own bodies.

Most women from Ballymun had their babies at St James's because of the weekly clinics that came to the health centre, or in the Rotunda, due to its close proximity to the 36 bus stop. I chose to go to St James's and it was there, all alone, that I discovered the 'delights' of childbirth.

There were two stages to go through; the labour ward and the delivery ward. Sporting a borrowed wedding ring and telling a well-rehearsed tale of a husband in the army who had been posted overseas to Cyprus, I joined the other married women as they walked the floor and rubbed one another's backs as the pain got steadily worse and worse. My mother rang in from the phone in the basement of Sean MacDermott Tower to be given the same answer every time, 'No change'. Apparently, it was only when the baby was actually born that they considered any sort of change had taken place.

Those women had lied. Those women who told me it was 'not so bad' had not even come close to telling the truth about how bad the pain of giving birth can be. Nobody had even mentioned the enema, the shaving, the waters breaking . . . or any of the horrors I learned of as and when they happened. These days *everyone* is aware of the physical feat of giving birth; we see it often enough on the TV (although I do think that is hardly a form of entertainment). But in early-70s Dublin the Discovery Channel was a long way off and the general way of finding out what childbirth was all about was to go through it, hour by excruciating hour. And I *still* feel that the worst part of it all was having to go through it alone, in the company of medical staff who knew I wasn't married, and did nothing to hide their disapproval of my situation. The people of The Mun may not have turned a hair at my situation, but the medical staff at St James's were not from Ballymun, and made it perfectly clear that they disapproved. Nobody had forewarned me that they could use scissors on me down there, and nobody had mentioned being stitched up afterwards. Giving birth at St James's hospital in the early 1970s was not even close to a nice experience, and nowhere near a beautiful one.

I had decided against the option of having an injection in my spine to numb me from the waist down, because I had heard of women who had that injection and never walked again. Everyone had warned me that I could end up in a wheelchair for the rest of my life if I went for this choice of pain relief.

To be fair to the hospital and its staff, they provided everything you needed for the ten-day stay in hospital that was obligatory after the birth of a first child (two weeks if you had a caesarean). Ready-made bottles were delivered to your bed, as were disposable nappies (which were quite the luxury back then) and anything else you might need, like . . . an ashtray—the little aluminium disposable ones that you used to get in McDonald's before they banned smoking.

There was nothing unusual about a mother feeding her baby with a bottle while her fag burned away in the ashtray on her locker. And in the evenings the babies were wheeled into the wards so that visitors could coo over them while they, too, smoked their cigarettes. Patients and visitors alike smoked in wards where little babies must have been gasping for air. While in hospital, the one thing you hoped visitors would bring you was cigarettes; after all there was little else to do during the lengthy stay. I remember a nurse coming into the ward one visiting time, waving her arms about as she walked across the room to open a window to let some of the smoke out while remarking frostily, 'It's like a tap room in here,' but she didn't ask anyone to put out their cigarettes. So you see, I wasn't the only naive one around at the time! The medical staff at the hospital were downright stupid! Now it makes the hair stand up on the back of my neck to think of those tiny little lungs, hardly even developed, having to breathe in foul, nicotine-tainted air.

A taxi took me home to Ballymun at the end of my stay in hospital, and I was bowled over when I walked into my bedroom to find the bed, the floor and every available surface covered in packages; gifts and cards to welcome my new child and congratulate me on becoming a mother. Little outfits, romper suits, cosy blankets, practical things like nappies and babygros, vests, bottles, a bottle-warmer, hand-knitted cardigans, booties and mittens . . . the list was endless. Not only friends but neighbours, the girls from Quinnsworth; so many people had gone out and bought or made gifts especially for my child that all I could do was sit on the bed and cry. It was a feeling that still makes tears prick my eyes.

The generosity of the people of Ballymun was boundless, and their acceptance of my situation was shown in many ways. People would stop me when I was out with the pram to admire the baby, and after every trip to the shopping centre for weeks after, I would have to empty the pram of coins that had been pressed into my baby's palm, 'For luck' just like any married mother. My becoming a single parent was something that has been happening to girls since time began, but only in Ballymun in the early 1970s could I have received so much acceptance of my circumstances.

In 1973 I drifted into a relationship and in 1974 I left Ballymun to set up home with him as his 'wife'. But things didn't work out between us, and when I returned to Ballymun a few years later it was to take up the offer of a flat of my own as the single mother of three that I was then. But in the few short years that I had been away, Ballymun had changed so much.

Chapter 3
The Rot Sets In

Returning to Ballymun on my own, with three children in tow, I was about to discover for myself how difficult it could be to run a household on the pittance the government thought was enough for a mother of three without a husband. My new flat desperately needed decorating, but it could have been worse. Someone I knew had been allocated a flat in another block that had been painted purple throughout. I don't mean just the walls, but also the doors, floors, ceilings, window frames and plug sockets. And not emulsion paint, but several thick coats of gloss paint that the Corporation had to come out and burn off before she could move in. Obviously, there was an element of undesirables already living in The Mun by that time.

The only furniture I possessed was a rickety old bed (which collapsed so often in the middle of the night that I eventually just put the mattress on the floor), two single mattresses for the older children and a cot for the baby. We didn't have so much as a cooker or a table and chairs for the kitchen at first. But the lack of a cooker wasn't a great problem, I just did what everyone else did at the time; I went to the ESB (Electricity Supply Board) showrooms in Fleet

Street and got an electric cooker that I was to pay for with my electricity bill, a little each month. I waited three weeks for that cooker, making do with a single-ring camping stove until it arrived (coddle followed stew, followed corned-beef hash for those few weeks). It was delivered at eleven o'clock one morning, and while the man wired it into the socket I started peeling potatoes and I had the dinner ready by twelve. Chips; I was beginning to think I would never taste home-made chips again.

My parents bought us a brown-checked suite for the living room (from a shop in Parliament Street; it cost £350, and they took on the weekly payments themselves so that me and their grandchildren could have a little comfort.) I made curtains with material purchased from Home Needs, rented a TV, and, little by little, our home came together. I have to say though, without the help of my parents I have no idea where I would have got furniture for my flat. The Society of St Vincent De Paul only helped out with the bare essentials like beds and blankets. I knew of many fatherless families who were not so lucky. But you made do with what you had, there were far more important things to think about than fancy furniture.

I didn't have any luxuries though, not even a washing machine, and with three children I certainly could have done with one. But, necessity being the mother of invention, I coped with the heavy laundry loads by soaking them in the bath overnight, then the next morning I would add some more hot water, roll up the legs of my jeans and stomp about on the clothes, kind of like a human washing machine. (Nobody ever had feet as clean as mine were back then.) That was the easy bit, then I had to wring everything out and rinse before wringing the water out again. Easy enough with socks and underwear, but not so easy when it came to jeans, sheets and blankets. It was to be another two years before I got my first twin-tub, a birthday present from my father, and it was sheer heaven to have a machine do all the hard work for me. The whites would go in first, then the light colours, and then the dark items. I can't help wondering now why I didn't put each load into fresh water. I think it may have had something to do with living in a caravan for so long that preserving water supplies was something that came naturally to me. Or perhaps I just couldn't be arsed with all the emptying and filling of the tub. I remember abusing that washing machine terribly; putting so much into the spin dryer part that I would often have to stand on the lid and jump up and down in order to close it.

There was still a lot of pride in Ballymun at that time. People still took it in turns to wash the landings and sweep down the stairs once a week. We kept the landings clean because that was where the children played when the weather was bad. And each week the caretaker would attach a hose to the hydrant at the top of the stairs to wash down the stairwells. The Corpo still sent the painters out regularly and the sense of community spirit was still very much alive. But other things had changed.

When Ballymun was first built all of the men who lived there had jobs. The first families to be given flats in Ballymun were allocated not by need, but by status. They had to satisfy certain conditions before they were given a tenancy; there had to be a husband, he had to have a job, and the couple had to have at least two children. Such discrimination would probably be illegal today. While China was telling its people that they could only have one child or they would be heavily penalised, Dublin Corporation was telling people they had to have two children, or stay homeless.

To the Corporation in the 1960s Ballymun was a model town, but by the time I came back in 1976 the situation had changed. The Mun was developing a reputation across Dublin, and it soon became difficult to achieve *anything* with an address in Ballymun. So if you lost your job, you were going to find it hard to find another one; to such an extent that by the mid 1970s there was a massive unemployment problem in Ballymun. I soon discovered that as soon as I gave my new address I would be turned down for any credit I asked for, and the only TV I managed to rent was one with a coin-operated box on the back, which had to be fed regularly with 50p pieces.

This situation was grossly unfair. The people of Ballymun were just that, people. Normal, generally intelligent people who were having their pride whipped because of the criminal element that was creeping into the place.

What made Ballymun start to change is not really all that difficult to work out. It was not only Ballymun that was changing, so was the rest of the world, in exactly the same way. All over the globe society was struggling to control levels of crime, drug abuse etc. And I suppose that it was not long before the criminals realised that Ballymun was the ideal place to conduct covert deals.

The very structure of Ballymun made it a haven for anyone who wanted to keep out of the watchful eye of the police. And as most of the children who had moved into Ballymun in the late 60s and early 70s were now teenagers, the drug dealers soon realised there was a huge market for their wares.

The warrens of the basements, 'the sheds', provided the perfect environment to sell drugs. You see, the basements in

Ballymun were not actually underground. They were at ground level; so the first floor of the flats was called the ground floor, the second floor the first floor etc. (which sounds confusing, but it wasn't when you lived there). Hence, although the seven towers were fifteen storeys high, the top floor was the fourteenth. Perhaps that was some-body's attempt at making sure that nobody ever *really* lived on the thirteenth floor, because the thirteenth floor was the twelfth floor really, and the thirteenth floor was physically the fourteenth. Originally, the basements provided storage (pram sheds) for anyone living on the top floors. But when it became clear that not only was nothing left in the sheds safe from the hands of thieves, but the rats that bred in the bin areas liked the warren of dark sheds too, they quickly fell into disuse. (I recall talking to someone on the phone at the bottom of Sean MacDermott Tower one night in the 70s, when a huge rat appeared in the main doorway. It stood staring at me, and although I tried to shoo it away, it was far too interested in me to leave in a hurry. A woman came through the passageway, saw the rat, screamed man's murder, and the rat legged it. Moral of the story: if you see a rat, scream like hell if you want it to go away. I wasn't scared of the rat; perhaps it knew this instinctively.) The Corpo used some of the basement rooms as maintenance sheds, offices and such. And some were turned into playschools that doubled as bingo rooms at night.

But the dark labyrinth of basements also provided all the cover a drug dealer needed. At first it was only pot that was readily available; and the police seemed to turn a blind eye to the use of hash. But then the real drugs came in; the speed, acid, heroin etc. and that was when Ballymun *really* started to change. The local chemist's shop was broken into several times by people addicted to, or seeing the huge profit in drugs such as Palfium (rich in opiates) and DF118s (Dihydrocodeine). In all reality, there was nothing going on in Ballymun that was not going on all over Dublin city at that time. Places like Dun Laoghaire had the same problems. The difference between The Mun and the rest of the city was that it was far easier for them to set up shop in Ballymun, and just as easy for those who lived outside the estate to drive in, buy what they wanted or needed, and drive out again, leaving Ballymun with the stigma of their addiction. And the media reports didn't help. I remember there being a huge drugs haul in Shanliss Avenue once, and suddenly Shanliss was in Ballymun instead of Santry. That's what the newspaper reports said anyway.

Police raids of any significance were rare. So when a friend of ours was at a party one night, on the seventh floor of Sillogue Road, and suddenly the police burst in through the balcony door, having lowered themselves down on ropes, it must have been a rather startling event.

She was taken into the bathroom to be searched by a ban garda who asked her, 'Do you have any drugs?'

'No, I don't take drugs,' my friend replied, horrified at the suggestion. The policewoman then asked my friend to turn out her pockets and place the contents on the side of the bath. This she duly complied with, and put her half-ounce of hash alongside her cigarettes and her Rizlas.

'What's that?' the policewoman asked.

'Hash,' my friend replied.

'I thought you said you didn't have any drugs.'

'I don't, it's only a bit of hash,' my friend replied.

Perhaps telling you the story of my friend's experience gives the impression that there were no junkies in Ballymun, only out-of-town dealers selling to out-of-town buyers; that Ballymunners only smoked a bit of pot. But sadly that was not the case. By their very nature teenagers are inquisitive creatures, and on an estate of twenty thousand people, it was bound to happen that some of them would end up living the life of the drug addict, and all that goes with it.

Burglaries became prolific on the estate. And nobody's home was safe. Many people who lived in flats near to the ground had metal grilles covering their balconies, and some even went to the lengths of having bars fitted to their windows. While the ground floor flats became easy targets, it was not unheard of for flats at the top of the towers to be cleared out, often in the middle of the day and via the front door.

A new item was being offered by the door-to-door sales people, who were quick to cash in on the booming security market that was developing in The Mun: spy-holes. Everybody had them. People became experts in the art of home protection and talked about the merits of mortice locks, spy holes and safety grilles over their pints in the Penthouse. It was on one of these boozy occasions that a friend of ours decided that he needed a steel door to keep the thieves out. Although they lived on the tenth floor of one of the towers, he and his wife had been burgled twice already; on one occasion when he was collecting her from hospital following a miscarriage. His reasoning was that if the Corpo used the doors to keep squatters out, they should work just as well against robbers. And so he 'acquired' himself a steel door; and then he got us one. Us? Yes, by then I was living illegally with a wonderful man who was later to become my husband and father to my three children.

One day, in the middle of the afternoon, I put some mince (even now I could write a book on 101 things to do with mince) on the stove and went down to the van (Nellie's) for a pint of milk. But when I got back upstairs I found that the barrel had broken inside the Yale lock, and I was firmly shut outside the steel-fronted door. (It was painted dark blue, and looked no different to the wooden doors of the other flats on the landing.) Realising the mince was on the cooker I began to panic, so a neighbour got his toolkit out and took off the door frame in the hope of getting to the lock, but no joy. Someone suggested that I run over to the police station, telling me that they had skeleton keys for all Yale locks, and I believed them. Honestly, you could tell me anything back then and I went for it. I ran across the road and told the garda on the desk about my predicament with the lock and the mince on the cooker and he told me not to worry, he would send someone over. I went back to wait on the landing for the two huge gardaí that were sent out to help.

I really *did* expect them to take a skeleton key out to open the door. I even had an image of what this key would look like in my mind. But, before I could stop them, they put their arms around one another's shoulders and barged towards the steel-plated door. I shouted 'NO!' but it was too late. They hit the door with every bit of weight those two burly men could muster, bounced off again just as quickly, and all I could do was call for the fire brigade as the pair went off to lick their wounds. So if you are ever locked out, and some fool tells you that the police have skeleton keys, do not believe them!

The Dublin Fire Brigade responded rapidly and got me in to the flat eventually, but not without a struggle. One unit turned up, but they soon realised they needed more equipment. So another fire engine turned up, the one that carried the hydraulic equipment they needed to get the door open. It was really embarrassing, standing there while people got out of the lift, looking at me curiously as they wondered what on earth was wrong that I needed so many firemen all at once. (While nothing to do with *The Mun*, I would just like to mention here what heroes firemen are. No other group of people put their own lives at risk to keep others safe to such an extent as the fire service; they should be paid their weight in gold!)

But when they *really* wanted to, squatters still got into empty flats, through the steel doors, without the aid of the Dublin Fire Brigade.

It must have been very hard for people living in squalid and cramped conditions with their children to know that there were flats sitting empty in Ballymun. Getting private accommodation in Dublin when you had kids was next to impossible. Private landlords seemed terrified that children would wreck their properties; so only those that landlords didn't particularly care about were let to families with children, such as caravans by the side of the Naas Road. (Although, that said, I am sure there must have been *some* landlords who would let their properties to families; I never came across any, but there have to have been some charitable, caring landlords in Dublin at that time, don't there?)

Flats with under-floor central heating and running hot water lay empty in Ballymun; and for some the dream really was still *that* simple, somewhere to live that didn't have mould growing on the walls and cockroaches in the cupboards. It was well known that once you managed to squat in a flat it took at least six months for the Corporation to get you out again. They needed a court warrant to get squatters out, and there were so many squatters in Ballymun that the cases brought by Dublin Corporation took that long to get to court. Of course, it was illegal for the Corporation to just throw a family out on the street when they had nowhere to go, so usually, inside a week or so, the family that had been evicted for squatting would be allocated a flat in their own right.

Now, don't go thinking I am on about hippy, druggie dossers here. In Ballymun families with children squatted in flats out of necessity. Squatting in a flat in Ballymun was simply a way of finding somewhere to live. The Corporation even accepted rent from squatters, making it even more important that they find the family somewhere else to live once the eviction notice had been served. However, before Dublin Corporation would allocate the evicted squatters a home of their own they first needed proof that the family *really* had nowhere else to go, a test related to the means tests of the 1960s. And the best way for most evicted families to prove that they had no alternative accommodation was to live on the landing outside the flat they had been evicted from until the Corporation came up with some sort of alternative housing.

(The *Sunday World* newspaper once ran a front-page report on how one of our soldiers was about to return from the Lebanon to find his wife and child living on a landing in Balcurris Road having been evicted for squatting. I think that must have been the fastest allocation of a flat on record as the Corporation bowed to public pressure and the soldier and his wife were given the flat next door to me in time for his homecoming.)

Everyone helped out at eviction times. Electricity was supplied via extension cables from adjacent flats, and neighbours took in the children, cooked meals, and shared bathroom facilities with the homeless until the Corpo came across with keys to a flat or a house. Squatting in the towers wasn't all that bad, as the landings were completely closed in. So once the family had been evicted, so long as they covered over the air vents, it could be quite cosy. But squatting on the balconies of the seven-storey flats, as some had to resort to, was not the best of places to be in bad weather. It was not unheard of for evicted squatters to wake up in the morning covered in snow.

Living on a landing, even if it was only for a week or so, was far from being a pleasant experience. While the community helped out, and nobody felt abandoned by their neighbours, it was still a humiliating experience for a family to have to announce to the world, 'I am so poor that I cannot even house my children.' Nobody thought that of course. Everybody just sympathised and felt an empathy with the family who were being treated so harshly by the state. These people were not asking for riches; all they wanted was a roof over their children's heads.

There was nothing romantic about sleeping on a mattress on a cold, tiled floor, with people stepping over your belongings as they got out of the lift. It was homelessness; and that's what it felt like. It was stupidity on the behalf of the Allocations Department of Dublin Corporation, who could have easily remedied the situation with just a little thought and forward planning.

The whole thing was like some sort of mad ritual; a three-ring circus performance during which it was essential for all parties involved to stick to the rules. The Corporation refused to lose face to the squatters, so eviction notices were followed by the bailiff carrying out the evictions, which always led to the allocation of another flat to the family that had been evicted. Why the Corporation couldn't just leave the families in the empty flats instead of going through an expensive court ritual is anyone's guess. But isn't that how it is worldwide, authorities making up their own rules and spending taxpayers' money to carry them out?

Now and again evicted tenants would wake up on their new landing home to discover that some toe rags had made away with the telly during the night, but those times were quite rare. Kicking a family when it is down is a pretty low thing to do. And to be fair, the only ones in Ballymun who were real low lifes were the junkies and the drunks that could be found on *any* street in Dublin. Most people were decent, law-abiding (we all have our goalposts on that one) citizens.

The couple that lived in the flat opposite ours were in the final stages of buying their own house on the far side of town, as they put it, 'As far away from this shit hole as we can get.' Meanwhile some friends of ours were living with in-laws, four of them to one room, and although the flat opposite only had one bedroom, it would be somewhere for them to be what they needed to be, an independent family unit in their own right.

But to squat in the flat it would be best to get there before the Corpo if they didn't want the trouble of getting in through the rusty steel door that would be in place once the flat was empty. Every morning I would look across from my kitchen to see if there were any curtains at the window of the flat opposite, planning to let our friends know as soon as they were taken down and the flat no longer occupied. But one morning I got the shock of my life. Not only were there no curtains at the window, there was no window at all! No glass, no frame, nothing but a big gaping hole.

I ran down the hall and opened my front door to find that the front door of the flat facing ours was gone. And when I went inside I discovered that not only was the window gone, so too were the taps, the toilet seat, the light fittings, plug sockets and every internal door, including the door that led to the balcony. The people across from us had moved out, and while we may not have seen them go, *somebody*

certainly had. With no front door to stop any curious child
from going into the flat, and potentially falling out of the
space left by the removal of the window (the bottom of the
casing was only a couple of feet from the floor), I had to do
something about it rapidly. I wasn't on the phone, I didn't
know anyone who was, and the phone at the bottom of the
tower had been nicked once again. So I ran as fast as I could
from James Connolly Tower to the Corporation offices at
the bottom of Thomas MacDonagh Tower, and fair play to
them, they sent men out to secure the property immediately.
Why someone decided to strip the flat of anything they
could remove, I don't know. Perhaps somebody was sick of
waiting for the Corpo to come out to do essential repairs
and decided to get what they needed themselves from
Corporation-owned property.

Whatever reason they had for their middle-of-the-night
salvage operation, it was downright bloody stupid of them
to leave the flat in such a dangerous state. Anybody else who
lived on that landing could have sent their adventurous kids
out to play, and any one of those kids could have gone out
that window. It's shuddering to think of, and utterly
mindless of the people who did that.

Anyway, as it turned out our friends *did* get to squat in the
flat, from where they eventually managed to be allocated
their own property.

Just the same, the Mormons never gave up on us. How many
times I opened my front door to find them standing there,
suited and booted like a couple of Stepford Husbands who
had lost their way; well, I never counted but it was *very*
regular. By regular I mean at *least* four times a year. The
American Mormons, from Salt Lake City, Utah, kind of
stood out in Ballymun. They were invariably around 6' 3",

with blond floppy hair, golden tans, and they always wore
suits, shirts and ties. They were the subjects of much ridicule
in The Mun, but if they noticed they just kept smiling
anyway.

'Hi, We're from the Church of . . .

'I know. Jesus Christ of Latter-Day Saints,' I would finish
their opening speech for them before reaffirming my
Catholic status and closing the door firmly. The representatives of the Church of Jesus Christ of Latter-Day Saints
seemed to view The Mun as a cesspit of sin, a contemporary
Sodom and Gomorrah, and they were desperate to save us
from ourselves. And yet, even though they saw The Mun in
the same light as an amoral town of the wild west, in the
opening years of the 1980s even they were not afraid to walk
the streets of Ballymun. So really, it can't have been as bad as
it was being painted by the media at the time.

We were in a friend's flat on the tenth floor of James
Connolly Tower one afternoon when a trio of Mormons
knocked on the door. But this time instead of being turned
away, Steve, my neighbour, invited them in. He smiled
mischievously as he came into the living room announcing,
'We have visitors,' with the Mormons following meekly
behind. Thinking about it, they must have been quite
shocked to be invited in so readily. They were thrilled to bits,
you could tell this by the beaming smiles that seemed wider
than ever. This didn't happen very often, and they were eager
to convert the Catholics to their ways. My friend Fran,
Steve's wife, kept offering them coffee, only to be told time
and time again that they didn't drink coffee. (All drinks
containing stimulants were banned by their church rules.)
So she tried offering tea, still a refusal. She finally got them
to take a glass of water each, but this situation did not suit
her Irish hospitality gene one little bit.

The Mormons told us all about the spirit world they believed in, where everyone who has died can live again, peacefully together with animals such as lions and tigers; they even showed us pictures of people having a picnic with a lion walking around in the background. And this was supposed to be a comforting image! They didn't seem to realise for a moment that with every question we asked we were taking the piss.

'What about the fleas?' Somebody asked the question that confused the blond, floppy-haired ones. 'I mean, if the fleas get to live in the spirit world too, wouldn't that piss the other animals off a bit?' But the Mormons assured us that even fleas can live peacefully in the spirit world. I think he was making it up as he went along myself.

'Tell me, these spirit people, do they go over to the other side as baby spirits and grow into big spirits, or do spirits stay the same age as they were when they died?' Steve asked a bemused Mormon, who promised to have that information for Steve by the following week. I began counting how many times one of them said, 'Ooooooh Kayyyyy', in a slow, American drawl. I got to 96 before it really began to grate on my nerves and I had to ask him to stop doing it.

'So what you're telling me . . .' my friend Steve had to be sure he was getting this right. '. . . is that, unless I become a Mormon I don't get to give up alcohol, tea, coffee, pot, cigarettes, Coca-Cola . . .' Steve stopped mid-sentence and waited for his words to sink into the brains of the missionaries. But they seemed a little stuck for words, so Steve carried on. 'I won't get to be dunked underwater in front of an audience while wearing a long white frock; I won't be able to pay for myself to travel the world to tell everyone else about the Church of Jesus Christ of

Latter-Day Saints . . . Man, I am sure missing out.' He finished, and the room erupted with laughter. But this attitude only seemed to make these guys all the more determined to save us.

We found it very hard to understand how *anyone* could follow that religion. Some bloke goes into a forest one day, God speaks to him and tells him to start this new religion where men can have as many wives as they like! Most people in Ballymun thought that these people were more than just a little bit bonkers. *We* certainly thought so, especially when we found out that the 'missionaries' had to fund their own trips to Ireland in order to 'save' the Roman Catholics. When they asked could they come back the following week we agreed readily. These guys were the best in-house entertainment we'd had in ages.

As arranged they came back the following week, and as agreed a few more friends had gathered at Steve's flat. But I think the whole thing must have been a bit too much for them that week, because they never did come back with the movie they promised us. We had a flat *full* of people waiting for that too. Oh, well, crowd—party—who cared about the Mormons?

A few weeks later I was walking down O'Connell Street with Steve and Fran when we saw the very same Mormons, standing in front of a huge banner, propped up against the wall. There were a few more of them that day (safety in numbers in O'Connell Street?) and a group of Stepford Wives were playing guitars and tambourines while singing one of those dreadful up-tempo songs that priests look on as 'rock music' when they allow it to be played in church. The 'band' formed a backdrop to the suited and booted ones who were trying to get people to talk to them in the street. They saw us coming, a brief discussion took place between them, and they quickly rolled up their banner, bagged their guitars and they legged it before we even got close enough to say hello!

In the late 1970s Ireland was very much a united Catholic country. Other religions were rare indeed. The Mormons may as well have gone to Australia to try to get koalas to stop eating eucalyptus leaves. Roman Catholicism was indoctrinated into the Irish people from birth, and there was no way a couple of weird looking dudes in suits were going to make so much as a dent in the shield that the Church was back then. People baptised their children into the faith within a couple of weeks of birth, because no parent wanted their child to die and end up in Limbo forever. And if there was one subject that most of Ballymun was united on, it was the care of children.

Chapter 4
Taking Care of the Children

If it was a peaceful life you were looking for, then Ballymun was not the place to choose to live. (Not that 'choice' came into the equation for most people.) By the early 1980s the Corporation had got around to providing some play areas for the children, with swings, slides and see-saws. Which was fine for the little ones who would play there for hours while their mothers sat on chairs over by the wall of the flats. But there was still nothing for the bigger kids. There were community-run youth clubs, chess clubs, etc, but nothing that kids really *wanted* to do.

There were children everywhere; well-fed, well-clothed, loud children who were sent to school every day by parents who knew the best way out of Ballymun was via the education system. But unfortunately, the education system failed many children in The Mun.

As adults we listen to people we respect, we learn from their knowledge and experience, and until our dying day we are all learning new facts and skills all of the time. But do we listen to, and take advice from, people we do not respect? Of course we do not pay any attention whatsoever to other adults who show us no respect; we would be mad, or very meek, to do so.

So what made the teachers of The Mun think that they could get any respect from the children *they* disrespected on a constant basis? OK, perhaps not all of them were vicious thugs, or looked down at the children they were supposed to be mentoring with the same respect farmers give to cattle being brought to market. Perhaps not all of them slapped children around the back of the head while calling them stupid. Maybe there were some teachers in The Mun who didn't make it perfectly clear what they thought of the children in their charge. Perhaps Mr Cotter didn't have a stick called 'Nelly' and he didn't keep that stick in the top left-hand drawer of his desk in his office marked 'Headmaster' in the Holy Spirit Boys national school. And maybe he didn't regularly beat the children he was supposed to be guiding through life with that very same stick. Did he really think he was instilling discipline by beating children with a stick or slapping them so hard across the face that he left an imprint of his hand on their little faces? Did he really expect to get some sort of respect from those children from the kind of brutality he meted out in his office? And did he ever get the clinkers out of his arse, or was it piles that had him constantly scratching his crack? There is *not* a fine line between violence and discipline, there's a whole bloody great chasm, but Mr Cotter managed to cross it effortlessly.

Mr Carroll was a teacher at the Comp during the 1970s; and he had a trick that helped him to catch many a first-year smoking at the back of the workshops. He would get a ladder and climb onto the parapet that ran between the main body of the school and the workshops; lean over the boys' heads and shout, 'You, you, you, get inside now!' as he pointed at each kid with a cigarette. If there was only one fag to go round, it was just unlucky if you were the one with it in your hand at the time. But one day his luck ran out when a passing student kicked the ladder as he passed by, leaving Mr Carroll stranded on the roof, desperately trying to get the attention of the canteen staff to rescue him. He must have been up there for a good twenty minutes.

There was one teacher who was awarded some respect by the kids in his charge: Mr McPhillips, the PE teacher. He was the kind of guy who gave a damn, the kind of person who could make a difference. He listened when the pupils had something to say, and the advice he gave was generally sound. A certain pupil (you know who you are) beat him up once, and the whole school sent this kid to Coventry because of it. It was injustice, and no true Ballymunner likes injustice.

I left school at the age of thirteen because I really could not take the humiliation any more. I could not take being treated as a fool by my teachers just because certain subjects would not sink into my head. The Irish language is something I never progressed in, past asking to go to the toilet and singing the national anthem. It just would not sink into my brain any more than maths would. It didn't make me stupid, it meant that I didn't care. I was never going to need to understand the Irish language, nor understand how you can possibly get the right answer to an equation with a variable in it. (I wouldn't normally tempt the God of 'Oh, Really', like that, but in this case I reckon I am pretty safe.)

To be fair to the teachers, they were not the only ones to instil terror into children; the Church joined in with the humiliation process too. Jimmy Murphy, an old friend of mine, remembers a day when someone wolf-whistled at a student teacher who was being introduced to the class by the parish priest. She only smiled, but the priest looked straight at Jimmy and pointed, even though he was wholly innocent of the crime and she hadn't seen who did it anyway. It came from his general direction and that was enough for the priest to draw his own conclusions as he carted poor Jimmy off to see the Headmaster.

Jimmy had a visit with Nelly too, but if he thought his ordeal was over when he left school that day, he was to find out otherwise later that evening. The priest stormed into the house, where Jimmy and his brothers and sisters were doing their homework while their parents were out getting the messages.

He looked at Jimmy like he was the spawn of Satan and snarled at him. 'Turn that television off right now,' he ordered, and the poor kids nearly fell over each other in a bid not to upset the 'mad' priest, which is how he was seen locally. He sat and waited for Jimmy's parents to come home and when they arrived he didn't waste a moment. He jumped to his feet and began a rant of abuse on the family.

'You want to learn how to control that little bastard of yours,' he said, pointing at Jimmy. And went on in a tirade about how Jimmy was evil, the only evidence of this being . . . well, no evidence at all actually. 'And he's probably one of the ones who wind up my dogs as well.' This particular priest had dogs who went mad barking at anyone who walked past the back of the parish house. But Jimmy's parents were not going to stand for that sort of behaviour in their house, and they told him so as they sent him packing. Even then priests seemed to think that they had some sort of divine right to tell people how they should be living their lives. And no matter how much Jimmy protested, the priest refused to listen to a word the '. . . lying little bastard' had to say.

It would be patronising of me to say that everyone in The Mun is intelligent, but has been given a raw deal by the education authorities. In every area of every country there is usually a balanced mixture of intelligence, and The Mun was no exception. So yes, there were the thickos who probably still hadn't learned much from life. That said, I have yet to find anywhere with such a number of quick-witted, lively people in any place I have lived before or since. However, even children who were exceptionally bright got little or no special attention from the teaching staff. Even a smart kid will eventually learn how stupid he or she is when told it often enough by someone who has a university degree and slaps the idea into place. Perhaps overcrowded classrooms made teaching a frustrating task in Ballymun. I cannot explain what made some teachers turn into the bullies they were any more than I can explain what made some saints.

When I left school I thought I was stupid and was destined to work only in shops or factories for the rest of my life, having been told that my dream of becoming a vet was unattainable to someone '. . . like you'. So I worked where I could, and when I had my children I didn't have *time* to think about working. I was uneducated. I could knit (including socks knitted on three needles), I could sew and I could cook. (Well, I thought I could, but apparently two tins of Heinz spaghetti in tomato sauce and a pound of mince does not make a bolognese.) I could reel off the names of every river and mountain range in Ireland and I could even baptise a new-born baby in the case of an emergency. I could recite prayers, I could run around like I was taught to in PE. But I had a very limited education in any of the skills that were likely to take me on to a decent career.

In many ways I got lucky. I managed to move to a quiet town, where my children got the education and respect from their teachers that they deserved. (There cannot be a prouder moment in a parent's life than when watching their children receive their degree wearing a black cap and gown.) Eventually, I went to college as a mature student, where I discovered that I wasn't thick after all as I got distinction after distinction for my work. When my tutor suggested that I take an IQ test I was astonished when I was invited to join Mensa. I say this not to boast—I gave up the pointless membership once I got over the novelty—but because there must be so many people like me who went through the Irish education system in the 20th century believing they were thick without ever getting the opportunity to discover or prove otherwise. As my friend Tina would say, many a beautiful rose grows from manure. The prisons of the world must be full of people who have used their intelligence in the wrong way, simply because some snotty teacher failed to recognise their academic potential. How many bright children the world lost out on because of the feckless attitude of teachers in Ballymun, I would not even dare to guess. All I know is that for the want of a decent education we have probably lost many a fine academic.

In the same vein; when my daughter's teacher, Mrs Kennedy, told me that she was the most disruptive child she had ever had the displeasure to teach, I was distraught. She told me that she was a nasty little girl and put her on report. I couldn't believe it, but I had to, after all it was a teacher who was making the observation, and therefore she *had* to be believed. Or so I was brainwashed into thinking. What baffled me was that at home she was a fairly quiet child. It was her brothers who were the boisterous ones. Then Mrs Kennedy left the school to go on maternity leave, and in her place came Miss Lamb. We felt somehow responsible for the way our child was misbehaving at school, and so we went to see the stand-in teacher to make sure our little girl wasn't giving her too much trouble. But when we explained why we were there she frowned at us.

'I don't know what you mean,' she said, seeming genuinely puzzled.

'Mrs Kennedy has dreadful problems with her,' we told her, and explained about how stubborn our daughter could be in class. But she shook her head. 'Honestly . . .' she told us '. . . she's fine. She does her work, and anything else that is asked of her.'

We felt thoroughly foolish as we left the teacher with her still wondering what the hell we were going on about. My daughter, although very young at the time, remembers the two teachers well, and although she was probably far too young to have acted as she did out of malice aforethought, she remembers well how much she liked Miss Lamb, and how much Mrs Kennedy's obvious dislike of my child brought nothing but contempt from the little one. Children do not learn from people they hold in contempt, even when they are too young to be able to spell the word.

I could go on for pages and pages telling stories of how children, in particular boys, were physically abused in school in the 'modern' town of Ballymun. I could tell you things that would make the hairs stand up on the back of your neck. But Ballymun was not much different from the rest of Ireland in its education system. But only in The Mun did kids have the opportunity to mitch so successfully. I would guess that when a boy didn't turn up at school at Blackrock College, his parents were informed immediately. When a boy didn't turn up for school at The Holy Spirit, Ballymun, nobody batted an eyelid so long as he brought in a note when he finally decided to return to school. Like the drug dealer, it was a lot easier for a child to hide in Ballymun than it would be on a nice estate in Dalkey. It is just a shame that so much talent went on to be wasted that might not have been in wealthier parts of the city.

Taking pride in how your children are presented to the world is not exclusive to the rich, and millions of yards of ribbons and tons of shoe polish must have been sold in Ballymun over the years. More than this, the children of Ballymun were *loved* children. Of course there were exceptions to the rule, there are neglected children everywhere. But those who knew how important it was to give children nothing but the best looked down on such parents. The myths perpetuating around Dublin about Ballymun being full of lowlifes was very far from the truth. Even when the bad elements of society were taking root around the estate, there was nothing happening that changed the way in which the majority of Ballymunners took care of their children.

There were certain rules you had to follow in order to be a good parent. Like the new outfit for the children at Easter and Christmas, not counted as gifts, but which had to be bought as well as all the toys. Christmas clothes were always the most special, and usually included a brand new coat. People would be putting money off the clothes for months at 5th Avenue, the clothes shop in the Centre; each instalment was carefully marked off on your card until there was enough money to tog out the kids from new underwear to topcoat. It was also very important that a little girl's hair was decorated with ribbons or bobbles to match her outfit.

It wouldn't be stretching a point to say that dressing the kids for Christmas and Easter brought out the competitive streak in us. And if you bought the kids' clothes in Arnotts, well . . . winner!

But when it came to dressing the kids for First Holy Communion or Confirmation times, Ballymun parents went bonkers, and often excessively so. Dressing a boy at such times was a relatively easy job: suit, shirt, tie, shiny shoes, a Communion medal on a rosette and you were done. But dressing a little girl for her First Holy Communion, now that was a whole different ball-*park* (we're not talking games here). When my little girl made her Communion I was no exception to the rule and it took me months to pay for the exquisite, Edwardian-style white dress that was a vision of ruffled lace, beads and fine stitching. But I didn't care what it cost; she was going to look beautiful, whatever the financial consequences. And the dress was not the only expense. She also needed the veil, the headdress, the bag, the parasol, the stole, the Communion medal on a gold chain, not forgetting the underwear, the hand-made socks and the pearlised white shoes that cost a fortune.

On the Sunday after my daughter had made her First Holy Communion we went into town, to Stephen's Green, where there were a number of families with children who had also just partaken of the Sacrament. And in my mind I can still see one little girl in the hand-me-down, yellowing dress, which her parents must have managed to convince themselves was a family heirloom, no doubt calling it 'antique' whereas I would have just called it 'old'. As my children stood by the pond throwing bread to the ducks, the little girl and her family walked by and the difference between how our daughter and the other child was dressed was startling. The little girl's dress was so old that it was yellow and her veil was limp. Her new, white shoes only served to emphasise the shabbiness of the rest of her outfit. As they went by, the parents of the little girl spoke to one another in what I can only describe as a 'posh' accent; they certainly were not North-siders. It wasn't just how they *spoke* that said they were not from anywhere near Ballymun; how their child was dressed said this for them. *No* parent in Ballymun would have turned their child out as shabbily as the well-spoken parents had.

We also had to save up for months prior to Communion and Confirmation times because it was (and no doubt still is) the done thing to go somewhere nice for lunch before visiting every friend and family member in order to collect 'Communion money'. Of course you weren't actually visiting to collect *money*; the purpose of the visit was so that the friend/relative could see the child on his/her Communion day, but the child always went away with money nonetheless. I would rather have left my rent short than short-change a friend's child on Communion day.

I know, I'm not mentioning the religious aspect of the Sacrament much. And I suppose that's because to the kids there wasn't much of a religious feel to it all (or was that just me?). Yes, there was the religious procession from the school to the church where the boys would sit on one side and the girls on the other, with their entire family in best bib and tucker beaming proudly at them. Yes, there was the Mass where Father Hanratty would drone on in his strange sing-song voice about the religious significance of the occasion. But in reality all the kids really cared about were the fancy clothes, the posh meal and the vast amounts of cash they were likely to gather. And again, there was a huge element of competition in how much you collected for your Communion or your Confirmation. So much so that parents would drag their kids all over Dublin, visiting relatives they had not seen for years in an effort to help out. Kids could, and probably still can, collect hundreds in one weekend.

To be a child in the late 70s in Ballymun was not a bad thing to be; not when you look at how bad some *other* places can be. Yes, kids went missing; but when they did nobody rested until they were found. I recall an incident when a young girl was assaulted and hundreds of people went out looking for the perpetrator; I dread to think what would have happened if they had got their hands on him. People simply did not get away with abusing kids in Ballymun. You might not have been keen to report a *crime* to the police, but nobody would have thought twice about reporting the abuse of a child to whoever they had to. Nobody would be called a 'grass' in Ballymun for reporting someone who was neglecting or abusing a child in any way. Nobody ever saw being hard up as any justification for neglecting a child. Many people in Ballymun lived on the breadline, but it didn't mean neglecting their children, it meant putting them first.

Some people reading this may find it hard to believe, but in spite of all the bad press Ballymun has received over the years, children reared there really *were* relatively safe. Yes, children got up to mischief, and of course there were accidents, but it would have been a brave pervert indeed to try to snatch a child off the streets of Ballymun. As the years went on and Ballymun's reputation became synonymous around Dublin with crime and drugs, the children were still protected by those who loved them, even more so when they could predict the dangers that were to come unless something was done to prevent it. Everyone in Ballymun belonged to a family, good or bad. Children knew one another, and so *people* knew one another. And people watched out for one another's children in a way that I have never experienced in any other community before or since.

As soon as the weather was good the mothers would be out with their chairs, and they would sit outside the basements in a row, watching their own children, and anyone else's who happened to be there. Of course, this was always the best way to find out any interesting snippets of information that were doing the rounds of the Ballymun grapevine. Gossip? Yes, but gossip is no more than modern-day jungle drums; it is a way of finding out what is happening around us. Gossip *can* be a bad thing, when the stories being told are untrue or harmful. But in general gossip is little more than communication within a community. After all, it's not so easy to hide what you're up to when everyone is talking about it. And in the early 80s you could count the real druggies who lived in The Mun on one hand. Even though there were swings, slides and climbing frames for the kids to play on, children did get bored and wandered off from time to time without anyone noticing. But even when a child *did* wander off, there was always someone to bring them home, or to the local police station, as was the case when my son went missing, aged two and a half.

I turned my back on him in Quinnsworth one day, to select some vegetables, and when I turned back he was gone. After a short, frantic search I discovered that someone had taken him to the police station, where I found him with a packet of crisps and a can of Coke, supplied by the kindly desk sergeant. I got a huge lecture on taking care of my child, and not an ounce of sympathy for my terror at having thought I had lost him. A week later he did the same thing again, only this time he found his *own* way to the police station in search of crisps and Coke. I couldn't take the embarrassment again and so I bought a pair of reins. But eventually I had to unhitch them; well it *was* time for him to go to university!

An uncared-for child was a rare sight in Ballymun. Great pride was taken in turning out smartly dressed, well-scrubbed kids. And in spite of what some people may think, many of the Ballymun kids went on to become successes in their own rights. (All my children certainly have.) Ballymun has turned out many professional, skilled and highly talented people. Sportsmen, musicians and writers who were reared in Ballymun are now living in all corners of the globe. In spite of the circumstances of their upbringing, and in spite of the lack of a decent junior-school education, many parents went on to become proud of their offspring's achievements. I guess that these results can only be attributed to the care those parents gave, in spite of all the difficulties.

In the early 1980s there were around 12,000 under-18s living in Ballymun; a vastly greater saturation of teens than in any other area of Ireland. And the vast majority of these kids went on to decent jobs and successful careers. For every teenager who got into trouble with the law in Kimmage or Walkinstown, five kids got into trouble in Ballymun. You see; it's not that the kids in Ballymun were any worse behaved than in other places, it's just that there were *more* of them, and it helped to be a hard nut when you lived in Ballymun. There are good and bad in all communities, and I would argue with anyone who said that the bad outweighed the good in Ballymun, because that was simply not the case. In the main Ballymun was home to young families, and in the main they were good people. And to be a child in Ballymun was to be blessed with memories funny and sad that they could not have found anywhere else in the world.

With so many children living in one place, the peer pressure was relentless. Kids in Ballymun grew up to be tenacious little characters, constantly in competition with one another so as not to hear the words, 'Cowardy cat, cowardy cat' chanted at them by the other children. The kids who were semi-educated together also lived together, played together and dared together.

I have recently found out about a couple of these 'dares'; apparently there was a hole in the glass of one of the sweetie counters in Jon's (Or was it Joe Wynn's? Those kids who told me this story are now adults who all seem to be suffering from diplomatic amnesia about the broader details) and I am told that all it took was a little distraction at the right time to get away with a handful of Bounty and Mars bars. From what I have been told I gather that this was quite a pastime for kids; so much so that I can't help wondering how Jon or Joe didn't cop on to it. Did they just think that Mars bars and Bounties were very popular sellers?

Before the Poppintree Estate was built, the farm that once stood there (Cod's Farm?) was also an attraction (or should that read *dis*traction?) for local kids. They would steal bales of hay from the barn, throw them into a ditch and jump in on top of them, over and over again. Eventually the bales of hay would start to break down, and the element of danger intensified. I am told that more than one leg was broken during this practice, which was called Jumping Jacks. And I suppose somewhere in the world there is now a grown-up who remembers inventing the name of this precarious 'game'.

A woman in James Connolly Tower once bought a mobile home with the intention of turning it into a shop van. This woman was not stupid; she knew that it would be overrun with kids before she could do anything with it unless it was secured properly, and nobody knows more about security than a Ballymunner. So, when she left it at the bottom of

James Connolly Tower the windows were taken out and metal panels were riveted in place, the door was firmly locked and a padlock added for extra protection. But she had forgotten one thing; the skylight. And this was how the local kids got in to strip the caravan bare before taking it apart from the inside out until eventually all that was left was the chassis. Not that I believe this was done out of malice. The caravan was not stripped with the intention of depriving the woman who owned it from making a living. It was simply something to do. It was good crack. It was play, Ballymun style.

A neighbour knocked one day to tell us that our youngest son had jacked his van up, front and back, with two scissors jacks, so that when he started it up the wheels just went round and the van went nowhere. The neighbour who had this practical joke played on him had to crawl underneath to let the van down again before bringing the jacks back to us. Why did my son do this? Because he thought it was a really funny thing to do at the time. To be honest, he still thinks it was incredibly funny to this day. He had nothing against the guy who owned the van; he was just having a laugh.

Another game my kids used to play, although I didn't know it then, was 'who can stop the closest to the wall on a bike with no brakes?' This entailed cycling as fast as you could, full pelt, straight at a wall, and using your feet as brakes. I now know that this is how my daughter's front tooth got chipped. I used to believe someone had pushed her off a wall.

Another, very dangerous, pastime was to ride on *top* of the lifts instead of inside them. They would get up onto the roofs of the flats and into the lift-shafts to wait until the lift came up to the top before jumping on board for a free ride. It's an absolute miracle that nobody was ever killed in this way, unless they *were* and I just didn't get that piece of news. If I had caught my children doing this they wouldn't have been able to sit down for a month!

Since I started to write this, all sorts of confessions have been coming from my children, my nephews and my nieces, who now find most of it really funny, while admitting they would go mad if they thought their own children got up to half of what they did. Like how when I first brought my children to live in the countryside after only ever knowing life in Ballymun, and they discovered the electric fences around fields, designed to keep cows enclosed. Much to the amazement of local children they would have competitions to see who could hold on the longest. And I also now know that when we first moved here my youngest son was famed for jumping into old, flooded abandoned mine shafts, holding onto breeze-blocks to see how deep he could get. If Ballymun gave my kids anything it was a sense of adventure tinged with danger, and the tenacity that they all still have to this day.

When we lived in Ballymun I was never away from Temple Street Hospital with the kids, for one thing or another. However, my kids were kind enough to have the sort of obscure accidents that nobody could have misinterpreted as child abuse. Like the time my daughter scalded her feet.

One morning as the kids were going out to play, I warned them not to go near the swimming pool because workmen were digging up the pipes outside, and the danger was obvious. Everyone was talking about the scalding hot water that was pumping out of the broken pipes down in the hole (yet another example of useful gossip). The contractors had gone and abandoned the hole for the weekend, covering the trench with heavy metal sheets, and it was an accident waiting to happen. But of course my kids took no notice whatsoever, and went straight across the road to see what all the fuss was about. My daughter, for some mad reason, decided it would be a great idea to run across the metal sheeting that the workmen had left covering the trench; one plate slipped, and she landed, up to her ankles, in the scalding water that was gushing from the pipes. I have no idea how she did not end up scarred for life, as the damage to her feet was dreadful. Were it not for the quick thinking of her older brother who pulled her out and removed her shoes and socks, I believe the damage would have been far greater. While his little friend ran all the way to the flat to tell us what had happened, he bravely carried her, and was half-way through the underpass when my hubby met up with him and took the heavy load that was our screaming daughter. For the next month I had to take her to Temple Street every day to have her blisters burst and clean dressings applied.

The poor little thing went through agonies, but we never did get to the bottom of who was responsible for leaving an unsecured hole in the road. We went to see a local solicitor who worked from an office upstairs in the shopping centre, and after investigation he told us that the Corporation were denying responsibility, and that a Dutch company had been contracted to do the work. I tried arguing that somebody must have *asked* the Dutch people to come over and dig the hole. They didn't suddenly wake up one day and think, 'Let's go dig a hole in Ballymun.' But responsibility was never admitted by anyone. These days I would tell such a useless solicitor exactly what I thought of his inadequacies before finding someone who could actually do the job in question. But back then I knew very little about the law, and when a legal representative told me there was nothing that could be done, I believed him.

My youngest son should have *lived* at Temple Street; it would have saved us a lot of money in bus fares. For years he had a permanent bump on the left side of his forehead; every time it would start to go down he would do something (like run into a tree, or play the 'bike with no brakes' game) to bring it back up again. He has a large scar under his chin today, owing to the amount of times he managed to open the same wound, which he originally got while playing on an old banger car that he was told repeatedly to stay away from. Eventually the car was set on fire. Not by a child but by the woman who had moved into one of the ground floor flats. She had quite a reputation for odd behaviour, not least of all hurling her furniture out of the window and over the balcony while raging about anything and everything, much to the amazement and amusement of onlookers. She had a row with the guy who owned the banger car, and in the middle of the afternoon she poured petrol over it and set it alight. She then set her flat alight before being taken away in an ambulance, never to be seen again.

One Saturday morning, when my youngest son was about three years old, I was woken just after eight by a knock at the door. A woman who lived on the ground floor, someone I didn't really know well, said to me, 'Now don't panic . . .'

Well, of course I panicked. Doesn't *everyone* panic as soon as they are told not to? I'm feeling panicky now just thinking about it! 'What?' I snapped when she didn't tell me quickly enough what I *wasn't* supposed to be panicking over, as the hot, burning feeling of dread was rising in my chest.

'Your youngest, he's out on the balcony, sitting up on the wall,' she said, and my breath nearly stopped.

I took off my slippers so that he wouldn't hear me approaching, and crept down the hall as quickly as I could;

terrified to distract him, I didn't dare call his name. I could hear him singing from the living room door; 'Ride a cock horse to Banbury Cross . . .' and he was still singing when I grabbed him from behind and hauled him off the wall and into the living room in one swift movement. I had thrown my slippers onto the sofa as I ran across the living room; and picking one up I reddened his little arse like it had never been reddened before or since.

I had no way of explaining to him the consequences of his actions. Three-year-olds do not understand the concept of death any more than they understand the concept of what could happen to a little human body at the end of a 180-foot drop. But what he did understand was that if he ever went near the balcony door again his backside would know the consequences. And I really couldn't give a damn for the argument against smacking children. I never have and I never will. OK, where it is appropriate it is far better to talk to a child about what they have done wrong. But sometimes, like in the case of my son and his balcony adventure, the only way to get the point across is a good slapping. Children who are slapped, in spite of the pathetic whinings of the anti-smacking brigade, do not grow up to hate their parents, and do not go on to become violent people. I don't condone violence, and nor do my grown-up children; I just believe that anyone with half a brain cell should be able to distinguish between cruelty and discipline. Slapping a child does not turn the 'victim' into a quivering wreck. If it did, then the children of Ballymun should all have grown into anti-social, intimidated misfits; but such was not the case. The anti-social misfits are, in the main, the children of 'liberal' parents; the ones who have never been given any real measure of how far it is acceptable to push the boundaries of social behaviour; the children who are given 'free will' without any understanding whatsoever of the concept. The children of Ballymun knew their boundaries, and in general respected the parents who laid them down. Lack of discipline is, in my opinion, neglect.

However, parental discipline did little to dampen the adventurous spirit of Ballymun's children. For example, gunners; now that was a strange one. Why it was called such is a mystery to me, and my kids can't explain it either. Apparently the pastime of 'gunners' entailed burning something plastic (milk bottles, old toys etc.) with a lighter or matches, and writing your name on the ground with the drops of burning plastic. My kids assure me that 'everyone' did it (Funny that, whenever I find out about something they did as children that makes the hair stand up on the back of my neck, my kids always assure me that 'everyone' did it. Like that somehow makes their childhood activities less dangerous.) and they were usually hidden out of sight in one of the many underpasses that were supposed to be used for people to get from one side of the road to the other. Not that the underpasses had been used for their intended purpose for many years. They were usually flooded, and the lights only worked up until the mid 1970s. By the late 70s only weirdoes hung out down there after dark and, other than the underpasses leading from the main roundabout, nobody used them during the day either.

Floods, now there's a memory. Nowhere in the world suffered from as many floods as Ballymun. The flooding of the underpasses was a simple case of blocked drains caused by Dublin Corporation neglect and heavy rains, but the flooding of the flats was a different matter. I know what you're thinking, Ireland can't *possibly* get so much rain that it would reach up to the ground floor of the flats. No, but the Corporation *could* turn the water off without telling anyone, and the scenario was the same all over The Mun; people would turn on their taps to find there was no water, and would forget to turn them back off again. Returning from a trip into town could mean returning to four inches of water in your flat and your belongings floating around.

And meanwhile, the only place to get fresh water at these times was in buckets from a standpipe in the basement (near the outlets for the rubbish chutes and the gigantic bins full of festering waste, where the rats lived) which then had to be transported back up to the flats. And when the lifts were broken, too, we began to have empathy with the people of Africa. Walking up 28 flights of stairs carrying two buckets of water is no easy task, not when that task has to be repeated over and over. And when you think about how far two buckets of water would go between an average-sized family . . . The stairs would be precariously slippery as people carrying overflowing buckets made their way up the concrete steps. Ah, yes! I used to feel great love in my heart for the Corporation as I trudged my way up the stairs with buckets of water—not! Generally, carrying water up the stairs, or even transporting it in the lifts, was a full-time job, so most people were at home, and aware of when the water came back on. But each time there would be a handful of flats in every block that needed to be swept out. And at such times it was all hands to the pumps.

Well, there *were* no pumps, pumps would have been very handy, but we had to make do with sweeping brushes and mops. All the neighbours would be out, sweeping the water out of the flooded flat as quickly as possible before it started to seep down through the hot presses (airing cupboards). Cascades of water were swept down the stairs and down the lift-shafts (and then we wondered why the lifts didn't work!) and the under-floor central heating took care of the rest.

The slums that were left behind for a bright new future in Ballymun.
(TLP/Getty Images)

Plenty of space to play, grow and thrive.
(National Library of Ireland)

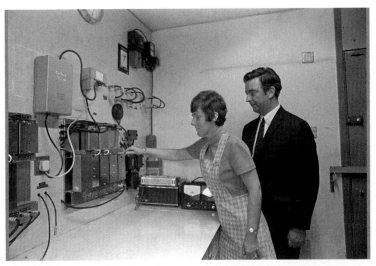

Switching on the piped TV, which was never quite good enough for my dad.
(RTÉ Stills Library)

Campaigning for contraception thirteen years before the legalisation of condoms.
(Derek Speirs)

There was always a queue for the phones in the shopping centre.
(Derek Speirs)

Girls from the Mun: facing the future.
(Derek Speirs)

Boys from the Mun: where are they now?
(Derek Speirs)

Divorce was as divisive in the Mun as elsewhere, compounded by the growing unemployment crisis of the 1980s. (Photocall Ireland)

Having the craic at the carpet seller's pitch at the end of Sillogue Road. (Magnum Photos/Martine Franck)

Filming Roddy Doyle's *The Family* in 1993.
(Derek Speirs)

A fortified van (shop).
(Derek Speirs)

On one occasion the water was seeping so badly from a flat on the fourteenth floor all the way to the seventh, ruining everyone's things that were in the hot presses, that, after banging on the door of the flooded flat several times, the Corporation men took the decision to sanction breaking down the door of the flat in question, only to find the occupant snoring in a drunken stupor, his clothes and other belongings floating around the bed. He got up, and wearing only red underpants, he sat on a chair in the kitchen, still in a drunken/sleepy stupor, while we swept the water out for him. When we were done he closed the door behind us without so much as a thank you. I didn't know who he was then, and I still don't know who he is now.

Another time a neighbour across the landing went out and left his taps on during a break in the water supply. We broke in, after making the decision to do so because it was what *we* would have wanted if we went out and left the taps on (I would have liked to have seen my neighbours trying to get through *my* door). Christy, the neighbour in question, had got his Christmas booze in, and we knew he wouldn't mind us having a beer for our troubles, it being thirsty work sweeping out a flood in a hot flat. One thing led to another, someone put on some music, and by the time Christy got in from his night out in town we had not only swept out his flood but had started his party for him too. But he didn't seem to mind too much. He just got himself a bottle of beer and started dancing!

There was *one* occasion when the Corporation were not responsible for one of my floods. I had left the twin-tub washing machine filling up and had gone next door for something. We got talking, and I was half way through my second cup of coffee when I remembered the washing machine. By then the whole flat was covered in about an inch of water.

*   *   *

The central heating in the flats was not under the control of the tenants. There were no thermostats, and what you got was what you lived with. (Hence the reason why the cold beer in our neighbour's fridge had been so tempting.) It was not only very handy for drying out floods but also for drying clothes; all you had to do was lay your washing out on the living room floor and it would be dry by morning. Although, in the days before anything resembling fabric softener, the drawback was that the washing was always stiff as cardboard when it was dried in this way. You didn't so much fold it as snap it into place. And while you may have needed extra heating in the summer, winters in the Ballymun flats were warm and cosy (so long as the heating wasn't off). It could be snowing a blizzard outside, but inside people were wearing shorts and T-shirts, and even then the windows would be open to try to get a bit of a breeze in. The problem was that above a certain height a slight breeze turns into a howling gale, especially when your flat is on a corner.

The windows were aluminium, and foam-backed nylon carpets were plentiful in the early 1980s. (Ballymun's best carpet/lino salesman at that time didn't have a store in the shopping centre; he simply set up shop next to the bus stop across from the swimming pool.) The combination of the two meant that every time you went to open a window the resulting static shock was inevitable. In fact, it was so bad in my case that I eventually got rid of the carpet in the living room, and replaced it with non-static lino, much better, easier to keep clean and far less trouble in times of floods.

Chapter 5
The Black Economy

Massive unemployment and the expense of bringing up children went hand in hand to produce a black economy that thrived in The Mun. Although, nobody ever *looked* upon it as a black economy. It was simply making a few bob on the side (doing a nixer). Doing the odd job so that you could afford that special First Holy Communion dress, that Confirmation suit, Christmas outfit or new school books. If you were on a low income you could get the books your children needed free of charge from the Eastern Health Board. But these books were never new, and every page was stamped: 'This book is the property of the Eastern Health Board', so no kid wanted to suffer the stigma attached to having free books. Sometimes there was no alternative for the parents other than to get these books for their kids; after all, education is far more important than pride, as most Ballymunners were well aware of. But usually you did whatever you had to in order to find the money to pay the cost of the textbooks that, like everything else seemed to go up in price every year. And of course, the older the child got, the more books they needed. It could be a crippling expense for some people who wanted nothing but the best for their kids, and where they lived didn't come into it.

So if you got the chance to make a few bob, well, it was quite acceptable. Apart from the time my youngest son decided to make a few bob by selling all my tapes on a door-to-door basis, at 20p each. This was one enterprise I could have done without. I had a hell of a job tracking them all down, and had to threaten one kid within an inch of his life to get back my *War of the Worlds*. Unfortunately, at the tender age of four my son was not very experienced in the art of sales and had started on the bottom floor, so by the time he got nearer to the top, where more people knew him, he had already got rid of a considerable chunk of my music collection. He knocked on my neighbour Marie Flynn's door and she thought he said, 'Do you want to buy some cakes?' until he pulled out what was left of my tapes from the pocket of his parka coat. She came and told me straight away, but by then it was too late.

And of course, I wasn't shy about making a few bob myself when the opportunity presented itself. These days my perception of right and wrong has adjusted itself somewhat to fit in with the rural surroundings I now live in. But in the early 80s I never thought for a moment that I could get into trouble with the authorities for making a bit of extra money now and again. It genuinely never entered my head that I was breaking the law during any of my little money-making schemes.

I had known my friend Fran for about two years when one day she announced that she could play the accordion. I'm not exactly sure how that one popped into the conversation; but off she went to get it. I expected her to return with a toy squeeze-box belonging to one of her sons, but no, this was an accordion all right. A ruddy great big one with knobs, buttons and straps. And it made a hell of a racket; it's amazing how loud a piano accordion is when it is played in a confined space. Much to my surprise, she could play it too. It was really quite bizarre to discover that the friend I had spent so much time with over the last couple of years had this curious hidden talent.

There was one small problem with her playing of this fine instrument; she only knew two tunes; Glen Miller's 'In The Mood' and Elvis Presley's 'Wooden Heart' made up her entire repertoire. However, she couldn't sing to save her life, so they were both instrumental versions. I announced that I could play the recorder (a skill retained since junior school), and dashed off upstairs to get the instrument that belonged to one of my children. Fran took out the sheet music to her two tunes, and I played along.

Now, I know it may sound a bit mad: 'In The Mood' and 'Wooden Heart' being played on a recorder and an accordion, but it worked, at least . . . I think it did. We came to the conclusion that, given a bit of practice we could go busking together, and decided to try it out on the night that the film *Annie* was being premièred at the Savoy cinema.

We sat on some steps between the cinema and the Gresham Hotel, and practised to a solitary audience of the taxi driver who was waiting for his fare in front of the hotel. A few bemused people passed by, staring at the strange girls playing Glen Miller music on a recorder and an accordion. Eventually the taxi driver came over and threw 50p into the hat saying, 'That's for your cheek, girls,' before driving off with his fare into the night, still chuckling. But we were not going to be put off by one philistine who couldn't appreciate true talent. We waited until the people in evening dress started to come out of the cinema, and struck up a furious rendition of both songs.

In our heads we had got this just right; where is the best place to entertain people who have money? Where the people with money are having a night out! It seemed wholly logical to us. However, what we hadn't realised, never having been invited to a film première, was that people don't bring money when everything is being laid on for them. One rather embarrassed man searched all his pockets before finding a 10p piece and throwing it into the hat that held only the taxi driver's 50p.

But were we put off by this experience? Not at all. We packed up and walked down O'Connell Street and, right outside the GPO, we started playing again. Perhaps our performance was so funny that people paid us for the laugh they got. Perhaps they really liked us. One way or the other, we earned £1.35p in five minutes before the gardaí very kindly told us that we couldn't do that sort of thing outside the GPO, apparently it was strictly not allowed since they'd had that bit of trouble back in 1916. They were very nice about it, and applauded our reasons for busking (to pay for school books) but they moved us on nonetheless.

£1.35p in five minutes, at 11 o'clock at night, worked out at an hourly rate of over £16. And that was with hardly anyone around. So, undeterred by our first busking experience, we bought some books of Irish ballads from Walton's Music store, and practiced like crazy until we felt we really were good enough to hit Henry Street in the daytime.

Fran came out with an old book of Christmas songs one day in June when we were practising in my flat. To make it all seem a bit Christmassier we decided to get a few decorations out. OK, so we ended up going a bit overboard and even put up the tree; but the atmosphere was great to try out the music to. There was a knock at the door, and when I answered it one of my neighbours was standing there, looking to borrow a fag.

Now, the thing you have to know about this individual was that he was a junkie, a heroin addict, and was permanently off his face on whatever he could get his hands on. But he was harmless enough, and remarkably intelligent for a man who had allowed himself to get into the state he was in. He had been writing a song, for years, and made everyone listen to it so often that I still remember it to this day. *I don't mind what you wanna do; it's all right with me if it's all right with you; I just wanted to let you know I love you. I don't mind what you wanna be, if it's all right with you, it's all right with me; I just wanted to make you see I love you.* (I wonder if he ever finished it before he died; it was such a good song.)

He followed me indoors and took the cigarette I handed him. He sat down and ripped it apart to roll a joint out of it, without saying a word, as we continued to belt out little numbers like 'Santa Claus is Coming to Town' and assorted carols. It was much later that we found out he was sitting there the whole time panicking; thinking: 'Oh man, I have lost six months, it's fucking Christmas.'

So that the neighbours would not suspect where we were going (for some reason we felt a bit embarrassed about becoming buskers at first), we packed the accordion into an old-lady-style shopping trolley, which also contained my recorder, sandwiches, a flask of coffee and all the sheet music we had, and set off into town on the bus. But by the time we got to Henry Street the pavements were crowded with shoppers and tourists and we bottled it. Instead of finding a spot in the busy street we ducked into the arcade that runs between Henry Street and the back of the GPO, and found a spot behind a pillar near the side entrance to Woolworths.

Things were going quite well; songs like, 'A Bunch of Thyme' work just as well for buskers as they have for Foster and Allen over the years, even when you don't actually sing. People put money in our hat and we were just starting to settle down a bit when we looked up to see a couple of blokes standing over the far side of the arcade. They both carried instrument cases, one with a fiddle, the other a guitar, and they were staring at us intensely. They had an unmistakable busker look about them. The cool-looking one in the black hat came over to talk to us.

'What you doing, girls? You know, you're in my pitch,' he informed us, at which point we immediately stammered an apology and offered to vacate his 'pitch' right away. 'No, no, you're all right, you're doing fine. We can go out onto the street. But stand out a bit, nobody can see you there, everyone is walking around wondering where that fabulous music is coming from.'

Fabulous music, and we could even have his pitch! Our confidence boosted by his praise we took his advice and stood out a bit, and allowed the acoustics of the arched arcade carry our music to the masses; who came by to give us some money, so much money that we could hardly believe it. And so busking became a daily event for the whole of that summer. The kids all got brand new books that year.

Eventually we moved our pitch and took up residence in the last doorway of Arnotts on Henry Street. This door was never unlocked, so we had the whole doorway to ourselves. We would go into town every morning with the shopping trolley and set up camp until 5 pm, when the security guard would give us a knock from inside the glass doors to tell us the shutters were coming down. The doorway is still there of course, but now there are solid, wooden doors where the glass once used to be. Eventually we brought in blankets, and cushions to sit on, and really settled in.

We tried to avoid blatant paramilitary songs, as many Irish ballads are, so we left out the songs such as 'Black and Tans' and 'Follow Me up to Carlow'. We wanted to cash in on the tourist trade, and didn't want to insult the English into not giving us their money. But we did perform 'Four Green Fields'; a nice little ditty about an old woman who had four fields, but strangers took one of her fields, but it was OK because she had sons who were prepared to fight to get her field back. Whenever we played this song people would hurl themselves in front of cars to get to us to throw money in the hat; so yes, we played it quite a bit.

The fabric shop that was next door to Arnotts (Hickey's) went on fire, and it was so badly damaged that a building firm were called in to make it good. One day, around lunchtime, a young lad who was working in there came out to speak to us.

'Excuse me,' he said nervously. 'But my boss said, would youse ever stop playing the "Four Green Fields" because . . . he liked it this morning.' Which I suppose means we played that song *far* too much, but hey, it was a money-spinner.

Always on the lookout for new material, we bought a new book of ballads from Walton's music shop, inside which there was an explanation of the meanings of some of the more ambiguous Irish folk songs. It was here that we discovered the meaning behind 'Four Green Fields'. The old woman = Mother Ireland; the fields = the four provinces of Ireland; the field that was stolen = Ulster; the strangers = the English; the old woman's sons = the IRA. No wonder people were dodging buses to give us money when we played that one. Isn't it unbelievable how naive we really were then?

This book also explained how 'A Bunch of Thyme' is a euphemism for a young girl's virginity, and the 'rose' mentioned in the song is the baby the sailor left the young girl when he took her virginity. Well, of course it is, once you are told this.

We really were quite good, and got better as time progressed. There must be heaps of video footage of us around the world. (A group of little girls once stopped and asked us if we were Charlie's Angels.) Tourists would stop to film us, and more than once we gathered a crowd.

One crowd in particular sticks in my memory as one we would rather not have had around us. We got into Henry Street one morning to find a young Traveller child sitting in our pitch outside Arnott's, singing some wailing old dirge. (My mother would call it 'The Tune The Old Cow Died From'.) The pitiful-looking waif, with a filthy face and matted hair that looked like it had been a long time since it was brushed or combed, was holding out a box to passers-by, and was taking what we considered to be our earnings. But she was only a child, so we asked her nicely if she wouldn't mind moving, explaining that we played there every day. She ignored us, never said a word and continued wailing out the tuneless lament. No amount of coaxing could get her to shut up and disappear. More than anything we wanted her to shut up—the dreadful sound she was making was GBH to the ears! Eventually I looked at her and growled, 'Fuck off,' and this got the message across nicely. She gave us a filthy look before darting off down the street.

We settled into our pitch and started working. But within minutes the girl was back, with a group of about ten kids in their teens, glue-sniffers, some still holding bags of glue, all with sores around their mouths, incoherent speech and stinking to high heaven.

Apparently two girls busking, surrounded by reeking glue-sniffers was something akin to entertainment in Henry Street that day, and a crowd gathered to see what was going on. We were shitting ourselves; I will not lie. This weird group of people were picking up our sheet music, trying to sing the songs, and generally making a nuisance of themselves. The stench of glue, campfire-smoke and body odour combined to produce a nauseating stench that made us fight hard not to retch. Drunks we knew how to deal with, but glue-sniffers . . . that was a whole new area of depravity to us. At the back of the crowd a middle-aged woman mouthed the words, 'Do you want the guards?' I nodded quickly, and she took off up Henry Street in the direction of the GPO. She must have fairly legged it because within seconds somebody said: 'Here's the guards' and the glue-sniffers dissipated into the crowd. The gardaí only stopped long enough to make sure we were OK before taking off after the sniffers. But ten minutes later they (the gardaí) came back to report that there was no sign of the glue sniffers. Itinerant children were pretty good at making themselves scarce when the law turned up. Moral of the story? Don't pick on kids!

Late one Friday afternoon a man stopped to listen and asked us to play 'On the Banks of My Own Lovely Lee'. We had the sheet music so it wasn't a problem. He was a big man, dressed all in black, and around him like a sash he was carrying a new inner-tube for a bicycle. After joining in for a couple of songs he declared he would be back the next week with his zither. Which was a statement that brought a little dread. If this man was a cake, he was definitely a fruit cake, one of those people who really seem to believe they are singing in tune (much like the Traveller child) when they close their eyes and get lost in the music.

That night Ellen, a friend who lived up on the next floor from me asked me to go up and meet someone she was 'eyeballing'. (The CB radio craze had firmly taken hold in Ballymun by this stage, and it wasn't unusual for a meeting to be set up following a few conversations [an eyeball].) We went upstairs, and lo and behold, the guy our friend wanted us to meet was none other than the man with the zither and the inner tube. He explained that he couldn't stay long, because he had a minibus full of young lads downstairs, he was their boxing coach. His CB handle was The Monsignor. And on the following Saturday night I nearly fell off my chair when Gay Byrne introduced him on the *Late Late Show*. It turned out he really *was* a Monsignor, and he was also a boxing coach, and he really *did* play the zither, but we never did see him again.

In general the gardaí who worked around the Henry Street area really looked out for us. But there was the odd one to watch out for. If a particular garda was on duty, though, you may as well just go home. He was one of those nasty officers, with a bad attitude, the kind that would give the whole of the gardaí a bad name. Another group used to play at the other end of Arnotts and when that particular garda came into the street they would be packed up and gone in seconds. But not us; usually the first we knew of the guard's presence was when two shiny feet appeared in front of us. Oh-oh!

We passionately hated the one-man-band and his pregnant wife too. He was one of those traditional one-man-bands with a guitar, a big bass drum strapped to his back which he played via a string attached to his foot, a kazoo, cymbals and any other instrument he could strap to his body and play so loudly that he drowned us out. Meanwhile the pregnant wife (who seemed to be nine months pregnant for the whole of that summer) was his bottler (she shook a hat under the nose of passers-by, something we never had the nerve to do). Once again, there was no point in hanging around while they were there.

When the summer was over, the weather grew colder and the tourists went home, we gave up on the busking and looked at other ways to make a few bob. And this was when the apple pies came into being.

With only a fiver we bought some cooking apples, some margarine, flour and sugar, and I made fifteen apple pies, which my husband took out in a box to sell on a door-to-door basis. I think he was only gone about half an hour with that first batch, which sold for a pound each, and yes, that's a healthy profit. Before long I was making thirty apple pies a day, which were supplied to shop vans around Ballymun, without a thought in the world for any hygiene or safety regulations. But don't worry if you were one of those who bought the pies; my kitchen was spotless. Although, that said, I usually had an ashtray, with a fag lit in it, next to me while I worked. It was years before I could eat another apple pie!

Being a mother of three on a limited income, learning how to knit and sew at school had not been such a bad thing after all, although I drew the line at knitting the woollen socks the nuns had taught us to make at school. I made a lot of my children's clothes, and would not have even *thought* about buying a cardigan or a jumper that I could knit myself for a fraction of the cost. I saw an advert in the paper for people to crochet shawls and applied for the job; two women came out to see me, liked the dresses and cardigans I showed them and gave me the work. The shawls were crocheted in natural Aran wool, and were destined for the Bord Fáilte shop at Dublin Airport. I must apologise now for any complaints they received about my shawls unravelling as they travelled home across the Atlantic, because I never did figure out how to finish them off properly.

I once bought twenty yards of blue, floral material at £1 a yard and made twenty little dresses and matching gipsy scarves edged in white lace (all for girls aged four because that was the size my own daughter was at the time), which I sold door-to-door at £4 each, again a tidy little profit. In Ballymun there was no need to find a gap in the market, produce a business plan, a cashflow forecast, keep books or any of those trivialities of setting up in business. With so many doors to knock on, there was always somebody to buy what was on sale, no matter how obscure.

Chapter 6

Just Passing the Time

Passing time in Ballymun always seemed to be easy. Doors were hardly ever locked, and friends spent a lot of time together. The parties were many, for any excuse, and often impromptu. Someone would pull out a guitar, someone else would go and get their guitar, bodhrán, banjo, tin whistle . . . and before you knew where you were the party would be in full swing. There was a time in the late 70s when the painters employed by the Corporation to revamp the landings were the guests of honour at one such party, and one of these painters never left again, and to the best of my knowledge is still living with the mother of four he met that night. I so hope they one day got to marry.

On one occasion the party in our flat (I cannot remember the specifics of the event) was well under way, and my other half had fallen into the (empty) bath, having consumed way too much Pernod and blackcurrant, and couldn't get out again. So I went into the living room for help to pull him to his feet. His mates pulled him to his feet, but he was out cold, so they decided that a bit of fresh air might help. The best way to bring him round, they concluded, would be to dangle him out of the window, by his feet! Only, they weren't holding on to his *feet*, they were holding on to his *boots*, and we were on the eleventh floor. He came to all right, with his brain trying to make sense of the upside-down view of the outside of the tower. Yep, that sobered him up quickly enough. If they had dropped him, well, there wouldn't have been many pieces to pick up. Reckless, yes of course it was, but it was funny too, and such was life.

There were very few old people in Ballymun, hardly anyone to tut-tut in disapproval, and with so many young people living in one place it was inevitable that they would behave as young as they were, parents or not. So there was hardly a night of the week when there wasn't a party on somewhere.

Johnny Logan won the Eurovision with 'What's Another Year', on the night of my birthday. Someone suggested that we turn on the TV to see how the voting was doing, and the cheers got louder and louder as good old Johnny was allocated scores of twelve after twelve. He wiped the board with the rest of the European competition, and we celebrated (with the help of the radiogram I had borrowed from my parents for the occasion) on his behalf until the early hours of the morning. (The following day my dad and my other half brought the radiogram home to Sean MacDermott Tower via the underpass beneath the central roundabout. Dad had unscrewed the legs and put them in his pockets to make it easier to carry, and because it was raining slightly I had covered it with a sheet. As they walked through the underpass a man coming the other way stopped, took off his hat, blessed himself and bowed his head as the 'coffin' passed by.) And, as usual, the kids slept through it all.

Kids brought up in Ballymun will sleep through anything. There wasn't only the noise of the neighbours to contend with; being only a mile or so from Dublin Airport, the planes flew overhead relentlessly, way into the night. Even at the top of the tower blocks you could feel the rumble of the Jumbo jets as they gained speed along the runway. But you learned to ignore them, and took no notice; apart from the night there was a power cut.

Power cuts were very rare in Ballymun. Being so close to the airport, the red lights on top of the towers had to stay lit so that pilots could see them. But on one occasion the power went, and the red lights went out too. While most people probably slept through it because it occurred at around 2 am, others were out on their balconies, lighting beacon fires so that the pilots of the incoming planes knew where we were. The airport was clearly visible in the night, and it was obvious that the power cut had not reached that area, and so planes were still landing and taking off. I turned on my radio to hear the song 'Who Put the Lights Out', and couldn't help wondering if the DJ was taking the piss.

This reminds me of the old (bad) joke:

Tourist bus going through Ballymun (OK, it's only a joke, no need to get technical.)
'What are the red lights for on top of the towers?' a tourist asks.
'To warn the pilots that the towers are there,' replied the driver.
'So, what are the towers for?'
'To hold up the lights!'

I told you it was a bad joke!

Christmas was one big party time in Ballymun. The parties started on Christmas Eve. Well, not parties as such, more like friends and neighbours having a few drinks together as they made the final preparations for the following day; put the bikes together, made the stuffing, laid out the new clothes etc. And the celebrations would continue all week, culminating in the best party of the year: New Year's Eve!

There was not much point in thinking of going into town on New Year's Eve, as that would entail engaging a babysitter and arranging transport (both equally difficult to get hold of on New Year's Eve in Dublin) and getting into a pub, let alone to the bar, in any part of Ireland was next to impossible. So the obvious solution was to have a party.

Usually it would be a 'Bring-your-own-booze' affair. People would stock up on bog rolls that week, and at the stroke of midnight the toilet paper would fly from windows all over the estate. Streamer upon streamer of cheap tissue would fly down the sides of the flats like giant ticker-tape, and people would yell to each other in greeting. The caretakers hated this tradition, mainly because they had to sweep up the mess the next day.

Because of this experience I was very much let down by my first encounter with the same night in England. At the stroke of midnight I dashed out into the street shouting; 'Happy New Y . . .' and my voice tailed off as I realised that the whole street was in darkness; everybody was in bed!

In the early 1980s it was still relatively difficult to get doctors to prescribe birth control. Fran went to the family planning clinic in town one day, having heard that the pill was easily available there. The pill was a relatively new phenomenon, and nobody knew very much about it, how it worked etc. A nurse asked her: 'Is it oral contraception you want?'

This was a query that Fran had not been expecting.

'No, I want the pill for ordinary sex.' She replied, wondering if there was something she had missed during her empirical sex education. Then, while her breasts were being examined the doctor said, 'So, you live in Ballymun.' And after a lengthy pause said, 'They are very high up. But I suppose they keep you warm in winter,' a statement which Fran took to be a physical reference to the position of her breasts, which were still under scrutiny, and in her nervous state it took quite a while for her to realise that he was actually talking about the flats.

Fran's husband Steve had given her a two-in-one—a portable radio/tape player—for her birthday. Which bewildered her a little because she couldn't quite work out why. We were particularly bored one day; just the two of us sitting drinking coffee while the kids were at school. So we managed to come up with the idea of making a tape of our own. Not music, actually I don't think that the notion ever entered our heads to record *ourselves* playing. I don't know which of us came up with the initial idea, but whichever one of us it was, the other obviously went along with the crack without any sort of cajoling, so I suppose we are both as guilty as each other.

The tape started with about ten minutes of silence followed by a sharp sound that sounded like someone knocking on a door, which was actually me knocking on the kitchen table. Another ten minutes of silence was followed by a crashing noise, which was Fran dropping a tray of stainless steel things (teapot, sugar bowl and milk jug—all empty) onto the floor. Again, a long silence followed by choking noises. (Yes, I will get to the point in a while.)

Steve came home at this stage, quickly sussed out what we were up to and joined in with the crack himself. Turning to his Wall of Sound equipment he plugged in a microphone and added to the 'fun'. More silent tape, followed by choking noises, followed by a little voice: 'Let me out, I'm choking in here, please let me out.' Followed by more choking noises. The finale was a booming, demonic voice: 'Let me out of the fucking oven!'

The tape machine was then hidden in the baking tin compartment at the bottom of the oven, plugged in behind the cooker, and we sat down in gleeful anticipation to wait for a victim. We invented *Trigger Happy TV* before Dom Joly was out of short trousers.

My eldest son was ten at the time, and he came home from school to become the target of our practical joke. We started our conversation about how it was a wonder the flats were not haunted as they were built on an ancient burial ground. Suddenly my son said: 'What was that?'

'What?'

'I heard a noise,' he said, and we duly sat listening for some time.

'Can't hear a thing; must be spooking you talking about ghosts,' I shrugged.

'No, *I'm* not spooked, there's no such thing as ghosts,' he said, so we carried on talking.

'What was that?' His voice sounded a bit more panicked at the muffled crashing sound. Because the tape machine was in the bottom of the cooker, the sounds were very muted and quite indiscernible. Again we waited and listened with straight faces, but there wasn't a sound, as we well knew there wouldn't be.

It was when the voice started that the panic really took hold and my son started to believe there really *was* something in the oven, something that had to be alive because it was talking! But, (OK, it sounds a bit cruel now, but it really was so funny back then) the more he panicked, the funnier we found it. I was choking with the laughing, with tears running down my face, and probably would have admitted the joke had I been able to catch my breath enough to actually speak. When he hurled himself at me for protection, and gripped on so tightly that he was painfully pinching the tender skin inside my arm, I still couldn't speak for laughing. (I'm feeling more than a little bit guilty as I admit this now. Although, he now agrees that it was really funny.)

Fran was in a similar state of hysteria to me, and Steve was out on the balcony threatening to throw up he was laughing so much when my other half came through the door. Our son babbled to his dad about there being something in the oven. His dad went over to the oven, opened it, looked inside and calmly said, 'Steve, what are you doing with a head in the oven?' as our son went into panicked frenzy. He had to be carried, kicking and screaming, over to the oven to have it proved to him that there was nothing in there. But he knew what he had heard, and so we had to take the tape out and play it for him to convince him it had only been a joke.

But the practical joke didn't only get kids. We scared the wits out of plenty of people with that one. One friend, Hub-cap (which was his CB handle) was so convinced that we had a tape hidden somewhere in the kitchen that he got up and searched the presses, the washing machine, and anywhere else he could think of that we may have hidden a tape machine. However, he refused to look in the oven. Really, what was he scared of? We got so much fun out of the spooky tape that a couple of weeks later someone decided it would be a good idea to repeat the process, only this time the tape machine was to be put inside a trunk and carried down Henry Street on a Saturday afternoon. That plan was abandoned when we realised that it might not be all that fair to scare the wits out of strangers. We should have done it; a few years later RTÉ ran a series of similar practical jokes. They even had a dead body sitting up in a coffin outside Donnybrook church as old people walked by. Now *that* just wasn't funny; someone could have had a heart attack.

On another day of boredom Fran and me came up with the idea of sending jam sandwiches to the neighbours. I would love to tell you *why* but I really don't have a clue. All I know is that it seemed like a really funny idea at the time. Fran had a huge box of envelopes under the bed (no, don't know why that was either) and we put a jam sandwich into about twenty or so of these envelopes, along with a typed quotation from the Bible, and posted them to the neighbours. Strangely, this did not exactly go to plan. The idea was that the neighbours would ask one another, 'Did you get a jam sandwich through your letter-box?' But nobody mentioned it; and the only evidence we found of our prank was an empty envelope on the landing of the eighth floor. Still with residue of strawberry jam inside, but the sandwich was gone!

Continuing with the practical joke theme, somebody once got hold of a shop window dummy. I'm not sure if it's the same one that was dressed up as a security guard and propped up against the Christmas tree in the middle of the shopping centre, (apparently several people had one-sided conversations with the 'security guard' that year) but great fun was to be had from the mannequin.

They who shall remain nameless took the fully dressed dummy, complete with hat, half-way down Sillogue Road one night. Then they put a rope around its neck and hung it from a lamp post, still wearing the trilby hat. They waited and watched from the sheds, and soon enough a garda came walking along, looked up, said, 'Holy Jesus!', blessed himself and legged it in the direction of the station. By the time the squad cars, ambulance and fire brigade got there, arriving almost simultaneously with their sirens wailing and blue lights flashing, the 'body' was gone.

'I swear to you, Sergeant, there was a body hanging from the lamp-post,' the garda said, looking up and down the snaking road to make sure he had got the right place.

'Well there's no*body* here now, is there? Unless you count us pack of eejits,' his sergeant said as he climbed back into the passenger seat of the squad car, and the flashing lights drove off into the night, much to the delight of the perpetrators of the practical joke who were still hiding round the corner, doubled up with laughter.

My next encounter with the same dummy was from my seat on the 36 bus as it stopped at the roundabout one afternoon. A group of teenagers were kicking and beating 'a man in a trench coat and a trilby hat', and the women on the bus, oblivious to the poor man's dummy status, were banging on the windows of the bus and standing up to shout out the windows at the 'assailants'.

'Let him go you little bastards, he's had enough,' they yelled as they banged on the windows so hard it's a wonder they didn't go through. The lads picked the dummy up and legged it, and the women all sat down in silence, realising they had been made fools of.

That dummy was indestructible. The next thing 'they' did with it was to wait until there were plenty of people around before hurling it from the top of James Connolly Tower, providing sound effects along the lines of 'Arrrrrghhhhhh!' as it tumbled through the air. Everyone who witnessed this really thought it was a genuine suicide. Strange how nobody considered the possibility that someone could have fallen by accident.

Ever needful of new forms of entertainment, some of our friends arrived at our flat one night with a German supply parachute. No, I have no idea where it came from, and I don't want to know. We tied all sorts of things to it before throwing it out of the window and watching it float down towards Sillogue Gardens, at which point our eldest son was dispatched to bring it back again. We had done this several times, not tiring easily of this new form of entertainment, when our son said: 'Do I have to? The lifts are broke.' The poor little sod had been running up and down the stairs all the time, when we thought he was getting the lift!

Sometimes a joke was simply too far-fetched: our friend Brian wanted to colour his little white Jack Russell with blue food colouring, strap a walkie-talkie to its belly and throw it out the window. His master plan was to knock on the door of one of the closest houses in Sillogue Gardens, hide around the corner, and via the other walkie-talkie say, 'Take me to your leader', when the door was opened. He got a few funny looks, but nobody was mad enough to join in with *that* one.

Although we *were* mad enough to go along with another crazy plan. Steve and Fran needed a bigger flat, and the one directly under us was coming up for grabs. But they didn't get it; they were told that they *would* have got it, but that this other family were higher up the list. Steve and Fran were desperate for the flat, so we came up with an idea that would make the new people ask to live somewhere else. I know that sounds harsh now, but we didn't know these people, and when you don't know someone, it's easier not to care too much. Besides, we reasoned that if our plan worked, the Corpo would have to give them somewhere else to live, so there would be no harm done.

Strike one. The new people had only been in their flat a couple of days. We had an old Sharp 40 CB radio, which was unique in that you could attach speakers to it and use it as a PA system. We didn't have any speakers, so instead we wired up a set of loud headphones to the CB, turned out the lights and lowered our 'PA speaker' out of the window.

'We know you're in there! You are surrounded, give yourselves up!' My other half shouted in his best culchie/garda accent, before hauling the speaker back up again. The headphones were surprisingly loud when there wasn't a head in between them. Leaning out slightly, we could see that the curtains below had been pulled to one side, and someone was looking out to see where the voice had come from. We heard the balcony door open and close, then went over to another window and repeated the process. 'It's the guards, come out with your hands up!' We only gave up when the poor guy stood out on his balcony, refusing to move until he worked out what was going on. By 2 am he still hadn't figured it out, and was still standing out on his balcony when we gave up and went to bed. Sorry, mate, whoever you were. Hope you weren't there all night.

We also staged fights, mainly in the bathroom so that the sound would carry down the pipes to the flat below, in an attempt to get the new people to move away from their rowdy neighbours, but they didn't work either. Perhaps the people who lived in the flat below us only got what they expected out of Ballymun. Perhaps our antics are partly responsible for the bad name Ballymun was getting all over town.

Chapter 7
Looking 'Down' on Ballymun

The media never let go of Ballymun for a minute, and it was a rare day when a *good* story was printed about the estate. The *Evening Press* and the *Evening Herald* constantly reported crimes that happened in Ballymun as though nothing bad ever happened anywhere else. Like the time of the drugs bust in Shanliss, Santry. People were becoming well sick of the stigma of criminality that was sticking to The Mun.

However, it is true to say that by the early 1980s Ballymun had changed so much that most people wanted out. Within ten years Ballymun had gone from being a model estate, filled with respectable families, to becoming a place where only the desperate wanted to live. New housing estates were being built in Clondalkin and Palmerstown, and this is where everyone wanted to live. (Ironically, Clondalkin was to go on to become just as bad a place to live as Ballymun. The only difference being that there were no high-rise flats.) Nobody was under any illusion about how difficult life in Ballymun was becoming, and apathy about living there took over. People didn't take turns at washing the landings any more, and it seemed as though all the caretakers ever did was wipe out the lifts now and again with stinking, black mops. The rubbish chutes were hardly ever cleaned, and I pitied anyone whose front door was close to the fetid waste-disposal areas that swarmed with flies.

You never knew what could come flying out of a window as you approached the flats: used nappies, TVs, sofas, bottles . . . And the date of 6 January was particularly dangerous as over the balcony was the best way to get rid of a shedding Christmas tree. I had disposed of my first tree by taking it down in the lift, spending an age sweeping up the trail of pine needles that I had left down the hall, across the landing, in the lift, and all the way round to the bins. The following years they went straight over the balcony. Not dangerously so, I always made sure there was someone at the bottom of the flats to keep people away so that I didn't skewer anyone. (Although I suppose being skewered by a Christmas tree *would* be an unusual way to go!) When the dairies started to put milk into plastic bottles they also doubled as excellent water bombs, as most local kids found out, making it even more important to look up as you entered the flats.

People were beginning to feel trapped in Ballymun. Not so much those families who lived in the houses, many of which had been bought by their tenants from the Corporation under the 'right-to-buy' scheme. But those families who lived at the top of tower blocks began to feel desperation as they watched neighbour after neighbour being moved away to shiny new houses on brand new housing estates.

In 1985, with the housing crisis worsening all the time, Dublin Corporation came up with yet another harebrained

master plan to deal with the situation. They offered five
thousand pounds to any tenants in Ballymun who were
willing to give up their occupancy and purchase their own
house elsewhere. This was a deposit for a house back then,
and many people jumped at the chance. Of course, this also
meant that a lot of people who were in full-time
employment left Ballymun; and that a lot of the long-term
unemployed moved in. Which is how The Mun ended up
with very high unemployment statistics.

It wasn't that the people of Ballymun didn't want to work,
more that the Corporation allocated so many flats to so
many people who were out of work in the first place that the
statistics were dramatically altered. It doesn't take much
thought to conclude that this could not be good for an area
that was already suffering from degeneration. But then,
when it came to Ballymun, the Corporation never did seem
to think in any lucid way.

Unless you or your children had some sort of severe
medical reason why the flats were unsuitable accommodation, you were stuck there. When I say *severe* I am not
exactly sure what definition the Corporation put on the
word. A family I knew had four sons suffering from cystic
fibrosis. They lived on the twelfth floor of a tower block, and
when the lifts were broken there was no other way home
than the stairs. But still the boys were approaching their teens
before the Corpo finally gave them a home on the ground.
Then there was a friend of ours who lived on the fifth floor of
a block of flats who couldn't walk without the aid of leg
braces due to contracting polio as a child. Like everyone else,
she had to walk up the stairs when the lifts were broken. This
woman should never have had to bring her children up
under such circumstances. Her disability was severe, and not
of her own doing, and allocating her a flat so high off the

ground was, in my opinion, a sickening case of 'couldn't care less' from the Corporation.

I knew many women who took anti-depressants in Ballymun. The strength of the Roche (as valium were known) was generally indicative of the strength of the problem. But it *was* depressing; it was depressing to live somewhere that nobody seemed to care about any more. Some tried to keep up the standards of the old days, but when nobody else was joining in with the landing-washing etc, it was hard to maintain.

It was discouraging to know that people looked down on you just because you came from Ballymun. We knew that we were just ordinary people living ordinary lives, but anywhere you went in Dublin you were looked upon as, not to put too fine a point on it, scum. Looking at Ballymun from anywhere else in Dublin made people feel safe, because they didn't live there. Because people only really had newspaper and other media reports to go by, it seemed to anyone living outside the area that Ballymun was Ireland's equivalent to The Bronx.

U2's Bono's well-publicised and, in my view, ignorant remark of how it was dangerous to walk in Ballymun at night did not help the area's reputation one little bit. Perhaps *he* wouldn't have felt safe in Ballymun at night on his own, but that was/is simply Paul Hewson's own paranoia. Of course it would have been unwise to wander down dark alleys in The Mun late at night. But so too was it dangerous to walk down dark alleys off O'Connell Street. Bono *never* lived in Ballymun! And yet website after website says that's where he hails from. Cedarwood Road may have had the same postcode as Ballymun, but it wasn't in The Mun. Now, I would understand the confusion if he originated in Ballymena; but how can *anyone* confuse the words Ballymun and Glasnevin? At some stage, somebody has given out that piece of information to the media. And going by the hundreds of websites I found that detail Paul Hewson's biography, nobody in Bono's entourage or staff bothers to correct this wrong piece of information.

I don't know *why* Bono found it necessary to comment on Ballymun in the lyrics of 'Running to Stand Still', a track from The Joshua Tree album; but perhaps I could be right in thinking that it gave him some sort of street-cred to associate himself with the estate he could see from his bedroom window in nice, safe, respectable Cedarwood Road in Glasnevin. All I know for sure is that when people in public arenas make off-the-cuff remarks such as his it is more damaging than helpful. Mentioning the seven towers in passing in one of his songs, '. . . I see seven towers, but I only see one way out . . .' was less than constructive. The lyrics beg the question: 'Really? And what way would that be?' Most people believe he is referring to suicide as the only way out; which is a nonsense suggestion as anyone who found other routes will tell you. But it doesn't take a lot of imagination to conjure up a scenario of an unemployed person, alone in a flat in Ballymun, longing only for the next hit, listening to that song and agreeing with what their hero was saying. Perhaps there are those who think my interpretation of those lyrics is wrong. Perhaps he meant some other one way out. The trouble is, I cannot imagine he is referring to getting a transfer to Clondalkin. Songs with lyrics about transfer lists are unlikely to have any popularity. The penultimate line of the song '. . . She will suffer the needle chill . . .' also makes me wonder if he could have meant that drugs were the only way out. I don't know. Who can say how the mind of a 'rock star' works? But I do know that the lyrics of 'Running to Stand

Still' are a portrayal of how the rest of Dublin felt about the estate.

It became increasingly difficult to be taken seriously with a Dublin 11 post-code. Jobs were hard to come by for anyone who lived on the estate that was mentioned in the papers every night of the week. And so many men joined the army, because only the armed forces didn't seem to mind where you came from.

Joining the Army in Dublin is not the same as signing up in other countries. Anywhere else a man/woman joins the army and generally goes away on service. Not so in Dublin. Men went to 'work' in their uniforms and came home again at night. The Republic of Ireland is a neutral country, and therefore doesn't go to war with anyone. Once the initial training is over, there is not much to do other than polishing your boots, taking part in border patrols, or going overseas with United Nations. However, any 'extra' duties such as these were on a voluntary basis, and the soldiers were paid additional money for them.

Soldiers were trained in the Wicklow Mountains, at the Glen of Imaal, and the tale of how someone shot a sheep by accident was told so often that if it were true there would not be a sheep left grazing in Wicklow. Yet another of those urban myths.

Ballymun had its fair share of soldiers, but then Ballymun seemed to have more than its fair share of most things, including some very clever people. One couple in particular, whose names have escaped my memory, carried out a scam that was very clever indeed, and as it was carried out against bookmakers, it didn't seem to be a bad crime at all. After all,

Rallying against the drug dealers.
(Derek Speirs)

Having a swinging time.
(Derek Speirs)

A horse leads a march against drugs.
(Derek Speirs)

Not what he thought the boss meant by 'a rise'.
(Derek Speirs)

Quick everyone—the lift is working!
(Derek Speirs)

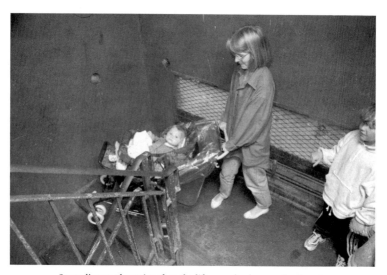

Struggling up the stairs when the lifts were broken was hard work.
(Photocall Ireland)

Was it just too much to ask for?
(*Irish Times*)

Trying to keep the children safe.
(Lensmen & Associates/RTÉ Stills Library)

Communion Day in Ballymun, with no expense spared.
(*Irish Times*)

After a while you didn't
notice the planes overhead.
(Photocall Ireland)

Graham Doyle: from the heights of
Ballymun to Home Farm and
Dublin City Football Club. (Inpho)

Demolition begins.
(Derek Speirs)

'Home'—no more!
(Empics)

New houses at last—all the
families ever wanted.
(*Irish Times*)

the bookmakers are happy to take anyone's money and make a fat profit. So the scam had a Robin Hood feel to it, more heroic than criminal. It wouldn't work these days, because everything is computerised, but in the early 80s it was a relatively easy scam to pull. I will use the names Dan and Jean to explain how it worked.

Dan would go to the local bookmakers and put a bet on, leaving a space in the middle of the betting slip. He would then go home and watch the racing on TV before getting out his carbon paper and filling in the gap on the betting slip with a reasonable winner, nothing too greedy that may have looked suspicious. Of course, he couldn't go back to the same betting shop to collect his 'winnings' because the ticket was numbered, and they would see straight away that he had filled in the winning horse *after* the bet had been placed. Instead, he would find a small branch of the same bookies, usually on the other side of the city, and go in there when he was sure they would be particularly busy.

Dan and Jean would synchronise their watches before he left for the other side of town and one minute before he was due to walk through the door of the small bookies Jean would tap the phone in the basement and pretend to be a counter assistant at the Ballymun branch. (Although the coin boxes had been removed from the tower blocks, it was still relatively easy to tap out the number you wanted to connect to, and many people, myself included, used these phones like their own private lines.)

'Hi, Ballymun here. Our board-marker has missed the non-runners for the 3.30 at Cheltenham/Ascot/The Curragh, can you let me know if there are any please?' Jean would ask. It was a common enough occurrence at bookmakers in those days and the person answering the phone would not suspect a thing, as she would go off to find the requested information. As soon as Dan was sure that Jean was on the other end of the phone he would then go up to the counter and act like he was in a big rush.

'Excuse me, can I cash this in here, I'm in a hurry,' he would say loudly, waving the ticket at the busy counter assistant who would invariably snatch it out of his hand before saying, 'this wasn't put on here.'

'I know, I put it on in Ballymun yesterday,' Dan would explain; at which point the counter assistant would remember that she already had Ballymun on the phone; handy.

'Can you give me a read-out for ticket one three five for yesterday please?' She would ask Jean after giving her the non-runners for Cheltenham. And after a rustle of a newspaper and a bit of a pause Jean would say, 'there's £120 to pay out on that,' and Dan would leave with the money. It really was that simple a scam. And they carried it out over and over until they eventually ran out of bookmakers.

Everyone knew they were doing it, but nobody cared. After all, the bookmakers were happy to rob the public blind day upon day. So who cared if Dan and Jean made the occasional £100? Of course, Dan and Jean are not their real names. If I could remember their real names I would not be able to write about their little scam here. There must have been bookmakers all over Dublin scratching their heads over where the money went.

What had once only been a black economy developed into an acceptance of criminality, so long as nobody got hurt. I don't mean to say that people accepted crimes such as mugging or burglary, but it seemed as though everyone smoked pot without even thinking about its criminal status, and everyone had an unlicensed CB radio.

* * *

Citizen's Band radio was just as good as a telephone in Ballymun in 1980. Because you could get your aerial higher than anyone else in Dublin, there was never a problem with getting a signal. DX27 and DX28 car aerials were attached to metal ground planes and fixed to balconies all over Ballymun. Some had fancy, custom-built ground planes fixed to the balcony wall, while others had biscuit tins. And one bloke we knew took the roof of a car up onto his balcony before realising that it was a tad difficult to attach to the wall.

As the craze took off people started to get really technical about their 'rigs' and before long The Satellite Seven CB Club was meeting every week at the church hall of St Pappins. It was at these meetings that vital matters such as who could modulate (talk) on which channels were agreed upon. One night there was a showing of *Convoy* to a packed audience, and even though the film kept breaking down, everyone had a great time.

To name all the members of that club would take a massive feat of memory; but to recall a few of the more memorable characters: Sledgehammer—fondly remembered as the instigator of the idea to sober up my hubby by dangling him out of the window. Another clear memory of Sledgie is the night we were all upstairs in the Penthouse after a club meeting and a fight broke out across the room. We just stayed where we were; the row was nothing to do with us. A heavy wooden chair came flying across the room in the direction of our table and Sledgie just put up his hand, deflected it back, and then carried on talking like nothing had just happened. I also recall Sledgehammer acting as chauffeur to a couple of CBers when they got married, tying white ribbons to the bonnet of his red Triumph Stag for the occasion. Sledgie was just one of those kinds of people; the kind that didn't mind helping anyone out when he could, in spite of his hard-man reputation.

Then there's Red Axle—Sorry, Red, but my memory of you goes back to the night in the club when you argued forcibly for channel 19 being reserved for 'truckers' only—I suppose driving a potato-delivery van was *something* akin to being a 'trucker'.

Starfish—he kindly took care of logistics when he called out every CBer in Ballymun to search for my son when he went missing one dark evening (the same son who used to find his own way to the garda station). That night, people openly used their CBs in a search that was, for once, carried out with the co-operation of the police. I'm not saying they physically went out searching like the members of the Satellite Seven club did, but at least they didn't arrest anyone for using their CBs that night.

Hot Chocolate, what can I say, if you don't remember him, you weren't there! And Ninja, another security man from Quinnsworth. He sang and played guitar and had the smoothest, mellowest voice I ever heard. He could have given Barry White a run for his money any day. Ninja had been a tailor once, and when I decided to try to make shirts for my sons he spent hours on the CB giving me instructions. Making shirts is something I never tried to do again; it is simply not worth the hassle. Ninja and his wife brought up six children in Ballymun, and each one of them was a credit to the lovely couple.

CBers in Ballymun were a little community within a community. Most people started out with a Sharp 40, which gave the basic forty channels necessary to talk to people locally, in Ballymun. But if you wanted to DX to the States or into Europe then you needed a rig that was up to the job. As time went on those who used the CB radio acquired the equipment needed to progress into transatlantic modulation (talking). The DX27s on biscuit-tin lids became Super Big Sticks, and the most lusted-after mike was the Ham Big Puncher. There were many conversations in the Penthouse and the Towers about the intricate wiring systems of power mikes, and people would spend days, sometimes weeks, going through the multitudes of wiring combinations there could be, but if it wasn't wired up to the rig correctly, it simply wouldn't work. Perhaps somewhere in the world there exist written instructions on how to wire up a power mike to a CB rig, but if there *were* any I certainly never saw them. Someone knew someone who could make linear amplifiers, which again boosted the signal, but the stronger the signal, the greater the likelihood of Italians coming in on the 'skip'. Now while I would love to tell you what this means in technical terms, I really don't have a clue. All I know is that as soon as we got a copy into America there would be an Italian there in the background somewhere. And invariably they couldn't speak English.

Today I can play mahjong with the Chinese or play chess with Americans, chat, send pictures etc, just with a few clicks of a mouse, but in 1980 we would spend hours and hours calling out for a copy into The States. 'CQDX, CQDX, this is Tango Charlie.' For some time we spoke to a guy called Mike 734 who lived in Long Island, New York, and we thought nothing of giving our address to complete strangers so that we could exchange cards, coins and sometimes small gifts.

Like the car number plate we received from Ray and June in Ohio that read, 'God made the Irish No 1'. The cards were displayed like trophies and there was great competition to see who could collect the most cards from the most places around the world. I believe that Ninja had the accolade for the greatest distance having had a conversation with someone in Australia; very rare indeed.

One night I really thought I had picked up one of my best copies ever, when the guy I was talking to told me that he was just crossing the Ganges on his way to the Himalayas. Weyhey! Was I impressed? Of course, it never struck me for a moment that this guy had an Irish accent; I guess it was just what I was used to listening to. It was only when I, very excitedly, told other CBers about this amazing copy and they fell around laughing that I discovered that, in Dublin CB terms, the Ganges and the Himalayas were the River Liffey and the Wicklow Mountains respectively. Well, how was I supposed to know? That's just how things were in the CB world. The Liffey was the Ganges, and the Gardaí were Bears.

We had a Stalker 9 CB radio, which developed a small problem in that it had to be hit on top before it would come on. As time went on it needed thwacking harder and harder to get it to come on, until eventually we kept a small hammer next to it. Inevitably it refused to turn on at all one day, and had to be taken into town to be repaired.

On the day that we picked it up we had gone into town with my mother to do some shopping. My hubby had the radio inside his leather blouson jacket (they were in fashion at the time), when we went into Arnott's for a cup of tea. And on the way back out of the store a moment of mischievous madness overcame him and he grabbed my mother by the arm.

'Excuse me, madam, I believe you have items in your bag you have not paid for,' he said loud enough to stop passers-by in their tracks as they stopped to watch the shoplifter getting arrested. My mother, being a unique kind of woman (I'm being kind here) didn't tell him to stop being so stupid and walk off like anyone else would have done. Instead she delved into her shopping bag and pulled out a till receipt.

'I've got my receipt,' she said, proudly holding aloft the strip of white paper so that the gathering crowd could see for themselves that she was an honest woman. My husband took the microphone of the CB out from under his jacket and spoke into it.

'64 to control. I have apprehended a suspect shoplifter at door number two, need assistance please.' As he said the words they sent my mother into quite a flap as she protested her innocence very loudly. And the crowd got bigger.

However, I don't think anyone actually noticed that he was also listening to the response of the unseen 'control' via the same microphone that he was speaking into. People were far more interested in the juicy bit of gossip they would be able to take home with them. Eventually my husband laughed, tucked Ma's hand under his arm, and we went off down Henry Street chuckling our heads off.

With so many CB radios in one area it was inevitable that the stronger the signals became the more likelihood there was of interference with other radio channels, such as the police and the emergency services. The AM radios we used to DX to The States were illegal but FM radios were less than useless and had hardly any range, so everyone ignored the government's attempts to get people to licence their rigs and move to FM radio, safe in the knowledge that it was next to impossible to be caught. To be caught using your CB radio after answering the door to a representative of the GPO accompanied by the gardaí would have been downright stupid. It wasn't illegal to *own* a CB radio, or to listen to it. The illegal part came into it when you keyed the mike and spoke to someone. And how thick would you have to be to do this in front of the authorities? So no, I don't recall anyone ever being taken to court for this *illegal* activity.

And I suppose using a CB with little or no regard for the legalities is yet another example of how easy it was to move the goalposts in Ballymun.

Chapter 8
Whatever it Takes

Obtaining what you needed by whatever means at your disposal could sometimes backfire. Like when a neighbour of mine was approached by a friend of his with an offer he couldn't refuse.

'Jimmy, I just bought a car,' Anto told him. 'But it needs some work doing to it, so how about I buy the bits, you do the work and we share the car?' It seemed like a good deal, Jimmy had a wife and two children, so a car would be an absolute bonus. And so he set about working on the Vauxhall Viva to make it roadworthy. He didn't know a lot about cars, so most of the work was carried out very slowly, with the aid of a Haynes manual. Every day, rain or sunshine, would see Jimmy downstairs tinkering with the engine of the little car. There were no garages, and so all the work had to be done out in the open.

One Saturday afternoon Jimmy answered his door to find Anto's little daughter standing there. 'Me Ma said Da's been arrested and would you go to the cop shop to find out why?' the child asked, and Jimmy duly complied.

'Who are you?' The garda behind the desk asked Jimmy when he enquired about Anto.

'His friend,' Jimmy replied honestly, and then got a bit too honest for his own good when he added the information: 'We own a car together.' A statement that made the garda's eyebrows raise.

'Do you now? Well, if you would just like to go through that door I will see if I can find out what's happening for you,' the garda said politely, and so Jimmy went into the little office next to the desk, to be met on the other side by the garda he had just spoken to. 'I am arresting you for Grand Theft Auto, you do not have to say anything but anything you do say may be taken down and used in evidence against you . . . turn out your pockets.'

Jimmy got a little more information than he expected that day. He found out that Anto had bought the car cheap from Travellers who lived on a campsite on the other side of town, without a log-book, with no receipt, and without asking any questions when he was getting such a good deal, or so he thought. The car had been stolen a couple of years previously, from someone in Ballymun who had recognised it as soon as he spotted it sitting at the bottom of the tower.

Both Anto and Jimmy ended up in court, and I have no idea how they managed to get off with the charges, even though they were innocent of *anything* other than gross naivety.

Jimmy was hooked on the car thing now, and he went out and bought himself a little Triumph Herald. But it had a blown exhaust, something that Jimmy could not afford to replace. Someone told him he should put a bandage on it.

'You're taking the piss,' Jimmy told his advisor.

'No, honestly, you can get a bandage for an exhaust at the garage.'

Jimmy could see that the guy was serious, but he didn't see the need to go spending unnecessary cash, so (without knowing that an exhaust bandage is made from special material), he went upstairs and tore up an old sheet. [You *know* this was not a good idea!]

With the bandage securely tied around the hole in the exhaust, Jimmy started up the car, and was quite pleased with the result, it really did seem as though the bandage thing worked—until flames started licking out from under the car, and Jimmy realised that the bandage had gone on fire, and the fire was spreading. The engine was still running, so quick as a flash he got into the driving seat and drove it across the road to the back of the police station. He got out and ran around to the front door of the station.

'Quick, there's a car on fire out the back!' He shouted, and the gardaí responded by grabbing fire extinguishers and running outside to put out the flames. They took the extinguishers back into the police station, but when they came back outside again, the car was gone, and so was Jimmy. In later years Jimmy went and got himself some real qualifications, and became one of the best mechanics around.

Like many people in Ballymun, Jimmy liked his hash. Some had their Valium, others had their booze, but Jimmy liked his draw. Short of a job to fill his time, and they wouldn't have him in the army (don't know why), Jimmy spent most of his days contriving new ways to smoke pot, and he didn't particularly care who knew. Like many other things in Ballymun, the misdeed of smoking pot was cast aside as inconsequential.

Jimmy had been trying to grow his own cannabis plants. He figured that with the heat in the flats all he had to do was sit it in front of the window to get some sunshine and he should have a bumper crop. But his plants grew to only a

few inches high, although they *were* green and healthy
looking. Then he heard about a cannabis plant that
someone had growing on his balcony in Shangan Road. It
was five feet high and nearly as wide (or so Jimmy was led
to believe) and to add insult to injury the guy who was
growing it didn't even smoke! Well, not weed anyway. So,
Jimmy, with hardly any encouragement from his friends,
who assured him they would be *more* than happy to share
the plant with him, set off in the middle of the night, with
an accomplice and a large black, plastic bag, in order to
liberate the plant.

While his accomplice waited in the shadows of the
basement with the black plastic bag, Jimmy carefully scaled
up the side of the balconies, heading for the fifth floor. But
when he tried to get a foothold on the fourth floor he
moved a paint tin and woke the occupant. When the
bedroom window opened and a gruff voice said, 'Who the
fuck is out there?' Jimmy had to make a fast retreat. He
scrambled back down and he and his mate legged it. They
got back home to find that Jimmy's friends had smoked the
little plants that he had given so much love and attention to
while he was gone, thinking that it was OK because they
would have a huge plant soon. Two days later Jimmy found
out that the plant he had tried to liberate had not been on
the fifth floor balcony at all, but the second floor, and he had
climbed right past it in the darkness!

There was a time, in the early days of Ballymun, when you
could use the balconies to store your Christmas booze
(nobody likes warm beer). But as the kids grew older and
became more daring (sometimes spurred on by the need for
heroin) scaling the balconies to rob the Christmas drink
became commonplace on the lower floors.

And it wasn't only flats that were being robbed. The Corporation had long since given up on the pay phones that had once been installed near the lifts in the towers. But eventually even the emergency phones were being removed as fast as they were installed, by a guy who worked for the GPO. He was selling them, and fitting them into people's houses as a sideline to his usual job.

When the heavy wooden doors started to disappear from the main entrance of one particular block of flats as fast as the Corporation could refit them, it was a bit of a mystery, until I was offered a coffee table that a bloke on the sixth floor had made. Apparently he was building all kinds of furniture, and the Corporation delivered him regular stocks of wood. I am sure these were fire doors, so how he was separating them and using what he had left . . . perhaps he will read this one day and tell us all about it. These doors, along with the doors from the landings, often disappeared at Hallowe'en too, when the bonfires stood tall all over Ballymun.

Hallowe'en was a magical time in Ballymun. All the kids would get dressed up and go trick-or-treating. Then there would be the parties for the kids with apple-bobbing etc. And no Hallowe'en would be complete without a barmbrack. At Hallowe'en in Ballymun you would find things in your barmbrack that the EU have probably since prohibited as a choking risk. Wrapped in greaseproof paper there would be several items that told your fortune. (Ireland's answer to the fortune cookie.) A stick—meaning you would grow up to be either a wife-beater or a beaten wife; a ring (always popular with the girls) which meant you would marry; a dry pea—you would never go hungry . . . I can't imagine for a moment that these prophecies were ever taken seriously, the kids would just laugh and gently tease the friend who was going to grow up to be beaten. At some stage of every kid's life they got the stick, the ring or the pea. And if the prophecies were to have come true, every child in Ireland would have grown up to be a violent, rich, well-fed person!

Returning to the subject of doing what you can to get by, another bloke was going all over Ballymun stealing the fluorescent tube lighting from the lifts and fitting them into people's kitchens. It was probably wholly his fault that the Corporation eventually put tiny little lights behind metal grilles in the lifts. At the rate they were disappearing he must have been doing a roaring trade.

I mentioned earlier how scary it could be to travel in a pitch-black lift; but the alternative of the stairs was a worse thought. Thankfully the lift never broke down on one of the blackout occasions, now that would have been terrifying indeed. By the early 80s the lifts were constantly getting stuck between floors, and we got used to having to spend whatever time it took to get us back out again. It was annoying, but you couldn't let it get to you too much when you still had to live there. More than once I have climbed out of a lift that the engineers had managed to move a little, enough for us to squeeze out, but not actually level with any landing. And when the lifts were broken, that's when shopping, babies, toddlers, prams and bikes had to be carried up the stairs.

By that stage, the stairwells were not the most attractive places to be, certainly not with young children anyway. The stairs of the flats that had once been swept by the tenants and hosed down once a week by the caretaker became a haven for any junkie or glue-sniffer who wanted to hide out from their parents or from the gardaí. And to pass the time while they were there they would urinate, vomit or paint the walls in graffiti. It became a common occurrence for used needles (often containing dried blood), glue canisters and other such refuse of degradation to be found on the stairs.

And who could blame the tenants for not wanting to clean up their mess? Caretakers were often lazy; (although some cared and still tried to keep the flats somewhere decent to live) and in general the pride they once took in their job was replaced by the apathy that was setting in all over Ballymun. The teenagers who used the stairwells as some sort of unofficial youth club (where nobody minded if they stuck needles in their arms, their groin or even their neck when the rest of their veins collapsed) even lit fires to keep warm sometimes, with no regard whatsoever for the safety of the families that had to live there. And when the rubbish chutes were blocked, people (ever faceless and nameless lazy bastards) would just throw their bin bags out on the stairs. Apathy, discontent and depression spiralled into a general carelessness about the estate. Inside, the flats were as well cared for as they had ever been. These were people's homes, and they were generally furnished and decorated to a very high standard. One of my friends even had her curtains made at Arnott's, and had a woman come out to finish off the hems in her flat.

The Corporation tried to get things back on an even keel from time to time. Like when they built high fences and gates around some of the flats, going so far as to put in intercom systems in an attempt to regain lawful order. But planners don't think like thieves or junkies, and they didn't realise that a fence, an intercom system, or even security guards are merely obstacles to be overcome. When a junkie needs something to sell in order to get the money for a hit, a fence is a minor detail. But like I said, town planners don't think that way. Even with the extra security measures put in place, Ballymun was still the best place in Dublin to hide out.

A middle-aged couple I knew had a guest staying at their flat. The husband, John, had met this bloke at work who had come over from England on a truck that was making a delivery to the company where John was employed. And when he (the English man) had expressed his intention to stay, John and his wife took him in to help out until he got on his feet, in a typically Irish hospitable way. The bloke said he was from Wakefield, and would be looking for a job and his own place right away. But weeks passed by and he didn't seem to be showing much interest in obtaining either. In fact, he didn't seem keen on going out at all, and was still there when I called one day, about a month after the Englishman had arrived in Dublin. John's wife was going to walk down to the ESB offices with me, where I intended to pay my bill, and when I called for her their 'guest' was laid on the couch watching TV, looking very much at home.

'Where are you going?' he asked without taking his eyes from the television, and I told him.

'Do you pay by cash?' he asked me, still not turning around, and I replied that yes I did.

'Does everyone pay cash?' he asked, and my radar switched on automatically. His interest in the ESB offices, and how much cash went in there every day was indicative of only one thing to me; he was thinking of robbing the place. It didn't take a mathematical genius to work out that so many bills being paid in one place meant that the office could hold thousands of pounds there on any one day. I didn't like what I was thinking; it didn't feel like he was planning on robbing the ESB office; it felt as though this man was planning on robbing the Ballymun people. These were people who so often struggled to get the money together to pay their bills in order to provide for their families, not to give this strange Englishman lining for his pockets. Worried about their safety, I asked John's wife to let me see his room while he was out one day. He had told John's wife that he was going for a walk, and I still reckon that he was sussing out the ESB office.

She wasn't happy about my intrusion into her lodger's privacy, but was glad she had allowed me to explore his room when a brief search of the suitcase that was under the bed uncovered a highly polished wooden box that looked like it could be a jewellery case. But when I opened it I found a set of shiny cut-throat razors laid on a bed of dark-blue crushed velvet. Looking a little deeper into the suitcase I discovered a British pilot's licence in a different name to the one he was using, and two British passports, both in names we had not heard before. Alarm bells were going off in my head big time, but John's wife was worried that if she went to the police and the bloke was innocent she would look dreadful. Especially as he had already paid that week's board up front. I pointed out to her that this man's actions were not what I would call normal; how he appeared to be hiding out, the cut-throat razors, the pilot's licence in a different name and the passports all added up to one very dodgy character. John and his wife were just an ordinary working-class couple, and they did not deserve to be used by this man in that way. So I went to the Garda station for them.

I told the police about the English man, and what he had in his room, and asked if they could look into it without me having to give John and his wife's name and address. The sergeant didn't laugh at me, but he certainly had an amused expression on his face. 'The thing is; if this man is dangerous, we really will need to know where he is,' he told me, and stood waiting, making it clear from his stance that he wasn't going to do anything until I gave him some more information about the situation. I sighed and told the garda what he needed to know. He assured me that if there were anything wrong they would let me know first. And he did. It didn't take long for them to find out that the man was indeed from Wakefield, Wakefield prison! He was on the run for armed robbery, and if I hadn't got suspicious of him he could have been hiding out in that innocent couple's flat for as long as he liked, such was the blanket of anonymity Ballymun could provide.

As the goalposts of criminality moved further and further in Ballymun, the playing field of the two sides, the people and the police, changed rapidly to accommodate the games. If you got away with driving your car without insurance, or not having a TV licence, it felt like scoring a goal for the right side. There was little or no liking for the gardaí that roamed the estate from the safety of their squad cars. And in all honesty, they only had themselves to blame.

When my oldest son was about ten years old he was playing in the fields at the back of the comprehensive school when his ball went over a wall. He looked over the wall, but it was a fair drop to the other side. However, he could also see a ladder down there that he would be able to use to get out again, so he lowered himself down the wall in order to get his ball. And that's all it was, a small child getting his ball back. So what the hell was in the mind of the young garda who brought him home to us that day?

My son tried to explain to the garda that he lived near the top of one of the tower blocks, so no, he was not trying to steal the ladder as it would have been utterly useless to him.

Just getting the fifteen-foot ladder up to the flat would have been next to impossible without help to feed it up through the stairwell. And even if he did manage to get it up to the flat, it would have been too big to keep anywhere but on the floor in the hall. The garda gave us his side to the story, my son gave us his, and I know which story had the most sense to it.

'Nice shine on your boots, how did you get them like that?' My husband asked the garda who was bright enough to realise that the subject was not something we wanted to discuss further, even if he wasn't bright enough to realise that a fifteen-foot ladder was of no use whatsoever to our small son.

In general, I can't really see what the gardaí were stationed in Ballymun for. All they ever seemed to do was drive around in their nice warm cars or, when the weather was good, set up checkpoints on the dual carriageway to catch motorists without tax and insurance. Whenever someone was burgled, robbed or assaulted they would turn up, ask all the right questions, take statements and go away. When Steve and Fran were robbed they actually asked them to '. . . let us know if you find out who it was.' No doubt someone has reams of statistics to show me that the gardaí really did solve crime in Ballymun, but like Mark Twain once said, 'There are lies, there are damn lies, and then there are statistics'. On the few occasions that I was actually in Ballymun gardaí station, I felt uncomfortable; in the way that anyone would feel uncomfortable when they are being looked on as a low-life. You can call that paranoia if you like; then you can talk to all the other Ballymunners who felt just the same way in the presence of the 'other side'. The gardaí alienated themselves from the community of Ballymun in so many ways.

Everyone who lived in James Connolly Tower or Sillogue Road knew old Frank. Most days you could see him at Nellie's van with his old shaggy dog. Frank liked a tipple, and most nights would see him singing his way home to Sillogue Road, his old dog waddling along behind him. Sometimes he would stop and sing in the one spot for a while, and someone would shout out a window, 'Frank, will you shut the fuck up and go home?' But he was a harmless old soul, and in no way deserved the treatment we witnessed him receive at the hands of the local gardaí one night.

We were in bed, fast asleep, when we were woken by a commotion outside. Our bedroom faced the back of Sillogue road, and when we looked out we could see that the commotion was Frank arguing with the two gardaí. Now, when you bear in mind that Frank was only a little man, when he swung a punch at one of the guards it was as effective as a two-year-old taking a swing at Mike Tyson. He missed, but the garda didn't, when he took out his truncheon and knocked poor old Frank to the ground. This frail little old man crumpled to the ground, his glasses falling off as he collapsed.

By this stage there were lights showing at windows all up and down James Connolly Tower and Sillogue Road, as people saw what was happening and protested very loudly at the old man's treatment. 'Leave him alone you bastards.' People shouted, but the gardaí ignored them.

Yes, Frank did take a swing at the guard; but there was no reason whatsoever for what happened next to have *ever* taken place. It was utmost cruelty, and even now it sickens my stomach to recall the barbaric scene I witnessed. It has left me with some mental scarring about police. Whenever I hear of someone suffering police brutality, the memory of

little Frank comes back every time. Whenever I hear someone say, 'The police wouldn't do that.' I think, 'Would they
not . . . ?'

Frank hit the ground with an audible thud, and the gardaí
grabbed him by his legs and started to drag him along the
Tarmac path. The pathway at the back of Sillogue Road
slopes, and every few feet there is a deep step. People could
see that they were getting very close to the top step with
Frank's head and they started really shouting at the police to
stop. But the gardaí took no notice, and Frank's head
bounced down the first step with a sickening thump. By this
stage the people at their windows were incensed and were
screaming at the gards to leave the old man alone. But again
they took no notice, and Frank's head bounced down
another step as the cries from the windows got louder. Frank
was a tiny man, and it wouldn't have taken any effort at all to
haul him to his feet and carry him to the station. But instead
they chose to drag the man by his feet, to humiliate him and
to put his life under threat. Eventually I turned away in
disbelief; I could watch no more.

It was a sickening, open display of police brutality, yet
who would dare to complain in person? The gardaí had
made it very clear what level of pain they were ready to
inflict on a harmless little old man; so who would dare take
on what they apparently had to offer? I doubt very much if
anyone ever put in an official complaint about Frank's
treatment. Nobody would have wanted to make personal
enemies out of the gardaí; besides, everyone knew that it
would be very unlikely for anything to be done about it. If
I were to witness such I scene where I live now I would
complain loudly and bitterly to the police authorities.
Men who actually investigate, and solve, crime in a
traditionally accepted sense, police the town where I now

live. The police in this town are human and friendly; and nothing like the personalities of the gardaí in Ballymun. But I doubt very much if anyone ever put in an official complaint about Frank's treatment. Nobody would have wanted to make personal enemies out of the gardaí, besides, everyone knew that it would be very unlikely that anything would be done about it.

And yet, to this day as soon as I see a police uniform I feel guilty, and I know I didn't feel that way *before* living in Ballymun. There was nothing even close to a relationship to be had with the local gardaí. They kept to their world and we kept to ours. And I suppose that when it feels like there are 'sides' it does no harm to the ego to know you have got one over on them from time to time.

The dual carriageway that leads into Ballymun used to sweep slightly off to the left before the new road was built, and it was just around this bend that the police would set up roadblocks to catch people driving without tax, insurance or driving licences. From our kitchen window we could see the cars slowing down as they came into sight of the roadblock, and you could almost hear the drivers say, 'Shite' as they rounded the bend. More than once cars tried to make a run for it by going up over the grass verge and trying to get to the other side of the road. But they rarely got away from the squad cars that would be waiting to give chase. There was never a feeling of, 'Good old gardaí, catching the tax-dodgers!' It was more a case of, 'Slimy bastards, can't be bothered going round the estate looking, so they set up a road-block!'

One night we were returning from a night out with a couple of friends when we drove straight into one of these roadblocks. We knew we were legally covered, but the gardaí took us out of the car and made us stand by the side of the road, in the pouring rain, just the same. I stood there without a coat, shivering, while one of the gardaí searched my hubby's pockets while the other searched inside the car, going so far as to root through the ashtray, looking for evidence of dope-smoking, I think. I was very tempted to ask the garda if he wanted a cigarette, but I kept my mouth shut. Finding nothing suspicious, they turned their attention to our friend Brian.

Now, for some reason, Brian had been saving silver paper at the time. He had heard you could save up enough to get a guide dog for a blind person, and he was really impressed with this. (Yet another example of a nice person from Ballymun thinking about someone less fortunate than himself, in spite of his own circumstances.) So, everywhere he went he would pick up any bit of silver paper he found and fold it into neat oblong shapes before taking it home and adding it to the huge ball of foil in his bedroom. However, when pot dealers cut cannabis into ten-spots, they are also sold in oblong-shaped pieces, wrapped in silver paper; so the garda thought he had found a real stash. Brian had about thirty of these silver rectangles in different pockets around his person, and as the garda went through them one by one the situation took on an amusing slant that really made standing there in the rain so worthwhile. The garda got madder and madder as wrap after wrap revealed nothing. It was very hard to keep a straight face as we watched him become quite frantic when he realised there was nothing in any of the little 'packages' after all. However, he had committed himself to the search, and probably working on the 'hide a pearl with other pearls' theory, kept us there until he had opened every last one of them, in vain. It was well worth the soaking we got for the entertainment.

* * *

With all the bank robberies that took place in Dublin during the 1970s and 80s, up until the time we left in the mid-80s, the banks in Ballymun had never been robbed. (Not that I can recall anyway.) I was standing at the bus stop one day when Sergeant Rush stopped to say hello. He had been making a bit of a nuisance of himself with a friend of mine, calling in for coffee when on duty etc, and he had stopped to ask me how she was. Standing talking to a garda in broad daylight at the bus stop by the shopping centre was not a situation that made me feel at ease, and I really wanted him to go away, far away. He mentioned something about a bank robbery a couple of miles away. Was he thinking I might have had some information on it?

'Isn't it funny how the banks out here are never robbed?' I said to him inanely, at a loss for something sensible to say. I never talk sense when I am nervous, and talking to him made me decidedly so. I couldn't just tell him that I didn't want to be seen talking to him. He was the only garda in Ballymun that I recall as being remotely human; he at least knew how to smile.

'Sure, why would they rob their own money?' Sergeant Rush replied, laughing. And I have always taken that as an intimation that he believed there to be more than one bank robber in Ballymun. Perhaps he was right, maybe there was, but I never knew of a bank robber in all the time I lived in Ballymun. The only armed robber I ever came into contact with was the one that had wheedled his way into John and his wife's home. And *he* was from England!

I have no doubt that in later years there were liaison officers, committees etc, who tried to get some sort of relationship going between the honest people of Ballymun and the local gardaí. But I doubt very much that any of it ever came to any constructive conclusion. If any such community liaison had been remotely successful, Ballymun would not be being pulled down now. So that's the answer to that question. Perhaps if the people of Ballymun had not felt bullied and intimidated by the local gardaí something could have been done to make The Mun into the decent place it should have been, but the reality is that most people felt alienated from a police force that seemed to be doing nothing whatsoever to halt the growing crime wave that was hitting the estate in the early 80s. People were scared, not for themselves so much as for the safety of their children.

There will always be exceptions to the rule in any context of life; and I have no doubt that there are some people in Ballymun who felt that they got along fine with the police. There are probably many people who can tell me how good the gardaí were to them in certain situations. Perhaps there *were* garda stationed in Ballymun who were kind, caring individuals who really gave two shits about the community they policed. But if there were, I never met them.

Chapter 9
The Corpo's Dumping Ground

The people of Ballymun objected to the way in which Dublin Corporation used the estate as a dumping ground for what they (the decent people of Ballymun) saw as degenerates and junkies. And they were right to feel offended by the attitude of the housing authorities. Everyone knew fine well that many of the people who were being housed in Ballymun would *never* have been give accommodation in a *nice* neighbourhood. What were the Corporation thinking of? In a period spanning ten years they had gone from being really choosy, only allocating flats on their model estate to families with an income, to putting any low-life into the flats that they (the Corporation) had neglected—and it looked like they didn't care so long as they got their rent. The whole of Dublin had the same opinion of Ballymun, that it was full of low-lifes anyway, so why should Dublin Corporation have had any better an opinion of their property?

People who lived in other areas of Dublin saw Ballymun as a veritable cesspit of human waste. People no longer came from all over Dublin to shop at Quinnsworth or for a night out at the cabaret room at the Penthouse. And eventually the Penter, as it became known locally, covered the dance floor with carpet and filled the space with tables, chairs and a pool table.

It is comforting for people who live in nice houses, on nice estates in places where the police actually respond when a crime has been committed, to know that they *don't* live somewhere like Ballymun. And from this comfortable position it is easy to believe the urban myths about how dangerous it was for an outsider to enter the estate. But let me tell you, there but by the grace of God go any one of mankind. At first people moved to Ballymun because it was new and exciting, but eventually people moved there only when they had to, when there was no alternative. That didn't make them bad people; that made them the kind of people who would live anywhere so long as they had a roof over their children's heads. And what the rest of Dublin seemed to forget was that, realistically, Ballymun was made up from people from all over Dublin. Only those actually born on the estate could consider themselves really as Ballymunners, and by the mid-80s only children and teenagers could claim to be true Ballymunners.

Because 45% of all single parents in need of local-authority housing were allocated properties in Ballymun by 1985, there was an urban myth perpetuating in Dublin that girls in Ballymun got pregnant deliberately, in order to get their own flat. This is nonsense of the highest degree. Girls do *not* go out looking to get pregnant in order to get a flat in Ballymun. And if any girl *did*, well, all I can say is she must deserve a flat in Ballymun at the very least if her life is so bad that she needs to resort to such desperate measures. Girls get pregnant outside marriage for the same reasons they ever have; love and ignorance. And marriages break up these days when relationships fall apart. Gone are the days when a woman would go to the priest with the problems of her marriage to be told to go home and make the best of things; that marriage is a sacrament, and cannot be broken.

As the single parents who were housed in Ballymun came from all over the country, it would be difficult to say what percentage of the single mothers in Ballymun actually came from the estate originally, but it is ludicrous to suggest that only girls *from* Ballymun ended up living in the flats as single mothers. By the 1980s girls no longer had to give up their babies for adoption when they were born outside wedlock, and welfare payments ensured that they could live a fairly decent life. But, and this is only my opinion, it seems as though those in authority still wanted to segregate unmarried mothers from the rest of Dublin, and the best way to do this, or so it seems to me, was to pack them all off to Ballymun. (At one time lone parents made up 37% of the tenants of Ballymun.) Dublin Corporation treated Ballymun as some sort of modern-day leper colony.

When it came to housing homeless, single people, once again Ballymun was the preferred choice of housing for Dublin Corporation, where up to 59% of all flats let to single people were in Ballymun. Many of these lettings were to single men who had been released from mental institutions and into the care of the community. In an ideal world people released from institutions would be able to make the transition without damage to the community they are placed in. But in the real world it is so often the case that these individuals fail to play any significantly positive role within the neighbourhood and are treated with, at the very least, suspicion by the community into which they are expected to assimilate. A little forethought may have made the authorities responsible for the housing of institutionalised men realise that if these individuals were to fit in with society in the outside world, it would be the world of the community they lived in. And unfortunately for many of them this was Ballymun, where people were protective about their children.

It's not politically correct these days to use words that may be offensive when talking about people with mental disorders. There was a time when categories of physical and mental ability gave a much clearer picture; imbecile, lunatic, spastic etc. Being politically correct was once a case of knowing not to call people such names to their face, but only in reference. But today anyone with any form of mental impairment is classed as having 'learning difficulties' by whatever degree; from being the kind of person who will forever be learning how to dress and feed themselves to someone who is a touch dyslexic. How is the term 'learning difficulty' supposed to explain anything to a young mother who is nervous of her new neighbour? Does it mean that the man has not got the ability to understand the difference between right and wrong? Could it mean that the man does not understand that it is wrong to molest children? Or does it mean that he has trouble with his spelling? For me, political correctness causes way too much confusion. And people are expected to be generous and welcoming to such people who are housed within their community, on the landings where their little children play!

One friend of mine had such a 'nutter' (her description, not mine) living across the landing from her. This man dressed as only someone mentally impaired could, he struggled to put a sentence together, and would stand at his front door watching the children as they played on the landing. It was when she found him in her little girl's Wendy house with her six-year-old daughter that she lost the plot and demanded that he was removed. He wasn't, of course. Social workers called to reassure her that the 'poor man' was harmless.

'You have him in your fucking street then,' my friend told the social worker. But of course the man didn't move away, and was still there when my friend moved to County Clare.

Such a welcome for people with 'learning difficulties' was never expected from the people who lived on Howth Head, or in any other affluent area of Dublin. In the main, it was the people of Ballymun who were expected to welcome 'nutters' into their lives.

It was not only people with learning difficulties who were released from institutions and sent to The Mun. There were also the people who had nothing wrong with them, but had been kept in institutions anyway because their mother had not been married. And some of these people, particularly men like Pat Tierney (I will get to him later) really made a valuable contribution to the community of The Mun.

When you put the statistics together with the fact that Ballymun only accounted for 10% of *all* local authority housing in the late 1980s, it is not difficult to see that the balance was not tipped favourably towards Ballymun and its people. The town was being used by the powers that be in a way that only served to increase the rift between Ballymun and the rest of the city.

People were scared. While it looked as though the gardaí either couldn't or *wouldn't* do anything about the increasing drug problems, parents lived in fear of their children becoming part of it all. And they were right to be scared. But they were ignorant too. I don't mean that they were stupid, I mean that this was a generation of parents who grew up to know socialising as going to the pub or to a party at a friend's house. Junkies were people who hid in the shadows in the 60s and 70s. They bought and sold their wares under cover of darkness; in secretive deals that they kept very quiet about. But in the 80s trade took on a different turn, and smack was openly being sold from flats all over Ballymun. The parents of Ballymun were becoming more and more isolated from a problem that was, paradoxically, taking over their lives, and they *had* to do something about it. Many of the people who were now parents of small children themselves had been the tenacious little characters who had grown up in Ballymun at a time when drugs meant pot, and you could count the junkies on the estate on one hand.

Getting rid of the junkies and the dealers out of Ballymun became pragmatic, and little thought was given to the circumstances of how the dealer got to where he or she was. But the sad thing is that *nobody* gets up one day and decides to become a junkie or a drug dealer. It is not something that any kid aspires to. The life of the heroin addict is not in any way a *good* life, and *nobody* would choose to go down that route deliberately, once again a, 'there-but-by-the-grace-of-God' situation. Children want to grow up to be train drivers and nurses. Never is it in anyone's game plan to take a road in life that can lead to one of the worst degradations known to man, and woman.

Whether it is because of peer pressure, excitement, or just a need to take the head away somewhere else for a little while, nobody ever takes their first hit of heroin with the intention of allowing the drug to take over their lives. When heroin is used for the first time, either smoked or injected, the user believes that he or she can just not take it any more if they so choose; that what they have just done was a conscious decision that can be reversed any time. There isn't a heroin addict alive who wouldn't like to give it up within a short while of first trying it. But by then it is often too late. Heroin use is very rarely a solitary activity. People take heroin in the first instance because they know somebody else who uses it, and the same goes for the somebody. And very often, in the early stages of addiction, there is little physical evidence of heroin being any harm to the user. They see their friends using it without turning into wretched junkies overnight, and people really believe that they can control the drug, and not the other way around. However, this is rarely, if ever the case, and as the body becomes tolerant of the drug, so too does it demand more regular use. The heroin user becomes part of a chain that consists of thieves, fences, dealers and other users. There is little point in a heroin addict trying to blend into society because 'normal' people don't want anything to do with them. But 'sticking to your own kind' only perpetuates the problem.

Once taken regularly, the heroin user soon finds that he/she needs to take more and more of the drug, just to feel 'normal'. Getting high becomes less of a need as the heroin becomes more of a medicine; to stop the shakes, the pain and the flu-like symptoms that the body goes through without its fix. Heroin addicts have to finance a need, not a want.

Communities within communities sustained by shoplifting, burglary, mugging and pick-pocketing wove a web of crime around Ballymun, until eventually nobody felt safe. Kids who had been reared in respectable families, who had successful futures ahead of them at one time, were drawn into an underworld where anything could be bought or sold for a price that was often very dear indeed. Heroin has no respect for family values, or family valuables. Doors that had once been left open so that neighbours could pop in and out of one another's flats were now firmly bolted. There was seldom time to get to know new neighbours, let alone get close enough to become real friends when thirty-five families were moving in and out of Ballymun every month.

It wasn't difficult to work out what was happening when queues of people would be going in and out of a particular flat. But what could anyone do about it? A woman on her own with her children may have been terrified that her kids would find an infected needle on the stairs, discarded by someone so desperate for a fix that they only got from the dealer's flat to the stairwell before injecting, but there was little else she could do about it but remove them herself. I suppose she could have gone to the Garda station and told them that she suspected a drug dealer lived next door; but what would that have got her, or her children?

I'm damn sure that I would *never* have 'grassed' a dealer in Ballymun, because as everyone knew, the dealers in Ballymun were little more than gophers (go-fors) for the drug barons who *didn't* live in Ballymun. When a heroin addict is desperate for an ongoing supply, and too tired, or too ill to continually steal to make money, the easiest option is to sell the drug, and when that addict is already living in the market, so much the better for the men at the top.

It is remarkably easy for a heroin addict to convince himself that he is carrying out a service by supplying a drug to people who would be very ill without it. Other users are his friends, and his friends introduce him to their friends, and so the life of the dealer is never a lonely one. It also has to be something of a comfort to know that there are so many others in the same boat; so many that dealers also manage to convince themselves that using heroin every day can't be such a bad a thing or so many people would not 'choose' it.

It is very difficult for anyone who has never known heroin addiction to come *close* to understanding how completely and utterly the drug can take over the life of an otherwise normal, law-abiding teenager. In general it is teenagers who try heroin for the first time. And, unfortunately, teenagers do not make the best master criminals. It is far easier to snatch a handbag from a woman taking a short cut home from the bingo than it is to rob a bank. Not to hurt the woman; because without the addiction to the drug the addict is more likely to be as caring a person as the next, but to satisfy a need that hurts so much. If you think that teenagers who mug and rob to feed their addiction care about what they are doing in any way whatsoever, well you would be wrong. Yes, in later months and years they *will* (if they live through it all) look back in abstract horror at what they did to survive. But at the time there is only one thing in the junkie's mind; and that is to stop feeling the way they do.

All of Dublin, and indeed the rest of the world, was in crisis over the drug problem in the 1980s, but nowhere seemed to be feeling the pain of it all more so than in Ballymun. Everyone knew someone who had been touched in some way by the heroin problem, be it as a victim of the drug or a victim of the crime the drug created. To anyone who has been mugged or robbed it may seem that I am being flippant in calling the drug users victims too. I am not, in any way, belittling the trauma suffered by people at the hands of druggies. But nor would I be so bold as to say I fully understand what decent people were going through. To fully understand what it feels like to have your cherished possessions stolen just so that a fool can get high is something that would have to be experienced first hand to fully comprehend. It must have been the hardest thing to come home to; to find that what you had worked so hard for was gone, and to know that the police were going to do nothing to help get back your precious belongings.

The gardaí paid lip service and filled out the essential forms. But everyone knew that they were not particularly bothered when someone had their Hi-fi or television nicked. It seemed as though there was always a car-chase going on somewhere; the gardaí seemed to like that part of their job.

One evening we were walking along the path that led from the end of Sillogue Road to Poppintree. It was fairly early, but already quite dark. The headlights of a car were heading straight for us along the path and we had to practically throw the children off to one side to prevent them being hit by the speeding car. It was very much a 'phew, that was close' situation. But, as we stepped back onto the pathway, barely having time to recover from the shock of the first car, we had to dive out of the way again as the squad car that was chasing it came belting towards us. It was out of the question for anyone to drive across that field legally, unless they happened to be wearing dark blue uniforms.

Unless they actually fell over any crimes, the gardaí in The Mun did little by way of solving them, as any amount of ex-Ballymunners who tried to get justice will tell you. Like the rest of Dublin, *they* didn't have to live there. Once their shifts were over, the Ballymun gardaí went home to their safe places and forgot all about the estate. It was up to the people themselves to pick up the pieces and carry on.

My friend Jimmy recounted a tale to me about something that happened to him and his wife one night in 1981. It is only a small incident, and nothing to do with the drug problem. But it shows what happened when a Ballymunner tried to do the right thing.

It wasn't late, around 7 pm. As Jimmy and his wife came out of the shopping centre and headed across the car park heading for Connolly Tower, they saw a young lad of about thirteen years of age, who had climbed up one of the flagpoles and was swinging on the rope in an attempt to pull one of the flags down.

'Get down out of there you little shit,' Jimmy told him as they approached, much in the same way as he would have done if it had been one of his own kids. Jimmy didn't go in for the destruction of property.

'Fuck off,' said the gurrier, holding onto the pole with one hand while repeatedly sticking two fingers up at Jimmy with the other.

Jimmy was reared in a time when you just didn't disrespect your elders, and he responded in the same way his own father would have done in the same situation. He grabbed the little shit by the hood of his Parka coat and hauled him down from the flagpole.

'Fuck off, fuck off,' the lad repeated over and over as he struggled to free himself from Jimmy's grasp.

Jimmy dragged the kid over to where there was a squad car sitting at the back of the garda station, with four burly coppers inside. They *seemed* oblivious to what was going on, and Jimmy had to knock on the window of the car to get their attention. They didn't roll down the window, but sat gaping at Jimmy like a pack of gormless eejits as he tried to convey to them, in some sort of convoluted sign language, the story of the kid and the flagpole

The boy, determined to get free, started kicking Jimmy in the shins as hard as he could. Of course, the gards couldn't see this from where they were sitting. All they saw was Jimmy's rapid response of sticking the nut on the kid in a head-jerk reaction. They were out of the car then all right. And Jimmy was hauled in through the back door of the police station while the kid who caused it all was told to go home. Yet another crime that the gardaí had simply fallen over during a tea break.

Jimmy tried to explain what had happened, but the young rookie with a face like a cheap pizza needed the bust. He needed every little bust he could lay his hands on to get transferred out of the hell-hole he worked in. (Of course, that is just an assumption of mine; for all I know he could have been really happy working in Ballymun.)

'What's your name?' He asked Jimmy when they got inside.

'Jimmy Murphy.'

'And who are you?' The garda asked, turning to Jimmy's wife.

'His wife,' Moira replied, indicating towards her husband.

'And what's your name?'

'*Mrs* Murphy,' Moira replied, in mischievous contempt of the rookie, and his treatment of her husband. The young garda turned red, and the bulbous spots on his face turned purple and threatened to excrete their contents.

'Don't go getting smart with me now.' He said in a broad culchie accent, loudly enough to make everyone in the room turn around, including Sergeant Rush, who came strolling over to see what the craic was.

'Jimmy, what's up?' he asked, and Jimmy recounted the tale of the flagpole, and the intense shin-kicking and '. . . I stuck the nut on the little bastard,' Jimmy admitted with a shrug.

Sergeant Rush laughed. 'Would youse ever go home out of that?' he said to Jimmy and Moira. And of course they did just that, leaving through the back door, eternally grateful for Sergeant Rush's sense of humour, the rookie still standing there with his notebook open.

We were fighting a losing battle. To Jimmy this incident was proof that there was no point whatsoever in trying to care about Ballymun when the police were not going to co-operate. OK, maybe he shouldn't have stuck the nut on the kid; but his shins *were* getting repeatedly kicked at the time. And in Jimmy's mind there was no longer much point in going to the police with something when you were likely to get arrested yourself. (Thinking about it now, it's nothing short of a miracle that John and his wife had not been arrested for harbouring a criminal when their armed robber was taken away.)

Jimmy grew up in Ballymun, went to school there, and eventually started work on the southside, in the catering industry. Jimmy had experienced the animosity that many Ballymunners felt from an early age: from the beatings at the hands of Mr Cotter and Mr Manning at the Holy Spirit Boys' National School to the beatings of the local gardaí. Jimmy knew that one day he would get out, and to the best of my knowledge he did. But I will never forget the stories he told me of how the Ballymun gardaí treated him on several occasions when his only crime had been naivety.

On one such occasion he was walking down Sillogue Road on his way home after working until 10 pm. He came across a group of lads who were around his own age, trying to get a motor-bike running. He put down his bag and helped them to push it, just as the gardaí came flying down the road with their sirens blazing and blue lights flashing. The police jumped out of the car, and without looking for any sort of verbal explanation jumped on Jimmy and started beating him with their batons. The other lads, the ones who had stolen the bike several hours earlier, legged it, and Jimmy was carted off to the station. He would probably have been charged with stealing the bike, in spite of his older sister going to the station to tell the gards that she had seen the lads with the bike hours before her brother got off work, had it not been for the intervention of Larry Duffy, a garda who was also a long-time friend of Jimmy's father from when they had lived in another part of Dublin. But incident after incident in Jimmy's life left him with intense feelings of animosity towards the gardaí, any many people in Ballymun were starting to feel much the same way.

The solution didn't take much working out; if the gardaí were incapable of doing their job properly, if the powers that be didn't know how to deal with the drug situation that was spiralling out of control, then the parents of the children of Ballymun would have to do the job for themselves. And so it was that the parentally-policed organisation CPAD (Concerned Parents Against Drugs) came into being.

Chapter 10
Concerned Parents Against Drugs

Vigilante—a word that conjures up a romantic notion for some, and a vicious vision for others. Some see vigilantes as nothing more than mercenaries who take money from ordinary folk; others see them as heroes, fighting the cause for the common man. They are generally perceived as hard men who stand in when the people are losing their fight against the baddies; be that a gunslinger in 19th-century Montana or a drug dealer in The Mun. The word vigilante is a label, whatever you perceive that label to mean. The trouble with labels is that they never have enough space for the full story.

I can't say I have ever had a lot of time for journalists. OK, there are things happening in the world that we need to know about, and without the help of journalists we wouldn't have a clue what was going on outside out own street (apart from what we got via gossip). I can accept that. But all too often reporters and editors embellish, exaggerate and twist the facts in order to create as sensational a story as possible in order to sell copy (which is a journalistic term for numbers of newspapers, magazines etc). And *that* is all about profit. Sensationalism is not always about who is sleeping with who; the media knows that there are certain words that grab the attention of the listener, viewer or reader. And 'vigilante' fits the bill very well as a word that grabs the attention in much the same way as 'pervert' 'scandal' or 'drugs', to name but a few of the words journalists use to catch the interest of the general public. (I'm sure there must be a secret book somewhere with an alphabetical, definitive list of such attention-grabbing words.) But to call the parents of the Mun 'vigilantes' is really stretching a point. In fact, I would go so far as to say that classing Concerned Parents Against Drugs as vigilantes is ludicrous. You will never hear the people of The Mun call themselves vigilantes, only the media does that, and only those who live outside Ballymun believe it to be true.

There is a fine line to be drawn between vigilantes and being vigilant; the words have the same root and yet have entirely differing definitions. So, when the decent people of the Mun got together and stood their ground against the drug dealers; were they being vigilant in that they were aware of whom the drug dealers were? Or were they being vigilantes in that they turfed the dealers out of their properties when they didn't stop selling their filth? I can't answer that question; I can only tell you as I see it; bearing in mind that I am not a journalist, nor would I ever aspire to be one.

As a parent I could see what was going to happen in the future in the Mun, just as any other parent could. But I was one of the lucky ones; I had a way out that wasn't suicide or drugs [as Bono suggested]. And so I got out of there when the opportunity presented itself. I didn't move to Clondalkin or Tallaght; but to a nice little town, surrounded by sheep and daffodils, as far away from the concrete jungle I had lived in for so many of my formative years as I could get. I needed to get my children away from there. And in some ways it was a good move; but in other, personal, ways it was the worst move; but in every way I still miss the Mun. And I know in my heart that had we remained in the Mun myself and my husband would have become part of the group: Concerned Parents Against Drugs. (Note the first two words of that group *Concerned Parents* not 'vigilantes'. It was *not* the people of The Mun who provided the label of vigilante; that one was down to the media.)

Parents did not know where to turn for help. No, that's not strictly true; they *did* know where to turn for help; but they didn't get it. Drug dealing was being marketed so openly that getting a list of names and addresses to give to the gardaí and the Corporation was easy. But getting the gardaí and the Corpo to do something about it; that was like pissing in the wind. Known drug dealers were openly named and shamed at public meetings where parents felt safe in numbers. The dealers were given the option to stop what they were doing or to get the hell out of The Mun. Some took the hint, some stood their ground, and some came to The Mun and blatantly set up shop. It became obvious that more stringent tactics would have to be deployed if the parents were ever to achieve any real results in their war against the dealers. It was these stringent tactics that gave the rest of Dublin the idea that vigilantes were patrolling the streets.

It's a different story when you live on a nice, tree-lined avenue in the suburbs. If someone in a nice area of Dublin is sure that one of their neighbours were dealing in drugs and went to the gardaí with the name and address, the house that had been fingered would be staked out and busted within a matter of days. But not so in The Mun; in The Mun it wasn't unheard of for queues of drug addicts to reach along the landing and down the stairs, while the gardaí drove by and watched.

There is no point in saying to a naughty child: 'Stop that or you will get a slap,' unless you are prepared to carry out the threat if the child continues to misbehave. Just as there is no point in telling a heroin dealer: 'Stop that or we will evict you ourselves,' unless you are prepared to go through with the forced expulsion.

From a personal point of view; if I were a heroin dealer in Ballymun and I were told to shut up shop or ship out, and I could see what was happening to those who refused to comply; what sort of gobshite would I have to be to hang around there? But apparently there were a lot of gobshites who decided to defy their eviction notices; and instead chose to turn their flats into veritable fortresses instead. They built steel cages that were fitted to the outside of their front doors. They locked their windows and put bars up on their balconies. But if they thought such measures would give them security from outraged parents who were hell-bent on protecting their children and their community, they were very wrong indeed. Like the battered wife who one day stabs her husband to death or the bullied child who one day takes the ringleader of the tormentors down, the people of The Mun, like the proverbial turning worm, kicked back.

From the outset, the decent people of The Mun had been kicked in the teeth. Firstly by the Corporation who failed to follow through on their promises, and allowed the town to deteriorate in ways they could have rectified with just a *little* sensible thought. Secondly by the gardaí who only ever seemed to pick on the residents who were, in the main, law-abiding people, as my sister-in-law and her husband discovered.

One night my sister-in-law and her husband were fast asleep in bed when gunmen burst into their flat. Their small children were tucked up in bed in separate rooms; the baby was in the cot next to their bed when they woke up to find guns in their faces. The gunmen forced the couple out of their bed, roused the sleeping children, and in between screaming and yelling, herded the terrified family into the living room. The children cried in fear, while their parents did their best to comfort their little ones; telling them everything would be all right. But in a little child's mind how on earth can everything be all right when there are armed men in the sanctuary that home is to a little kid, waving guns around like they are taking part in the *Gunfight at the* OK *Corral*?

The gunmen had chased a man into the flats. Unfortunately, my sister-in-law's husband had forgotten to lock the front door that night; so when the gunmen chased their quarry into Sillogue Road flats they tried every door from top to bottom. In their adrenalin-fuelled frenzy they took the unlocked door to mean that their intended prey had not had time to turn the key, or was too smacked off his face to remember to do so. In their haste they presumed that he had stripped his clothes off and got into bed quickly in an attempt to evade their 'justice'. They instilled abject terror into that innocent family that night, in nothing more than a case of mistaken identity, for, it transpired, they were armed gardaí.

My sister-in-law's husband had got undressed that night and hung his clothes up as he usually did. His clothes consisted of the uniform of the Irish Army; a uniform he was proud to wear; and never more so than when he had stood guard over the body of Eamon De Valera. These men, who could also be called 'vigilantes', had got it wrong; but I don't suppose that's what the report said when they went back to the garda Station with their tails between their legs leaving a distraught young couple to pick up the pieces. (If indeed such a report was ever filed.)

Men (fathers, older brothers, uncles and grandfathers) took shifts in standing guard at the entrances to the flats. They would challenge anyone who looked suspicious, and turn away strangers who looked as though they may be there for their supplies. In my opinion this is not the action of vigilantes, this is the action of taking security measures to protect your own children. Parents will do anything within their physical and mental power to protect their children. It doesn't matter if they live at the top of a tower block or in a stately home in the country; parents still feel the same way about their children. Parents would lay down their lives for their children; so why should it be wrong of them to stand up and fight the deadly threat that heroin was to the young people of The Mun? That's an easy question to answer, no it is never, ever wrong to stand up and fight when your children are being threatened. There's a saying I like, 'If anything is worth fighting for, it's worth fighting dirty for.' I don't know who said that, but when it comes to fighting for children, no parent would consider any fight too dirty. However, in a world where there are police forces, no parent should ever have to.

Think about it for a moment; no matter where you live in the world you should be able to get the support you need from the local police to get rid of illegal drugs traders. But when that support is not forthcoming what are you supposed to do? Of course, if you lived in the 'right' areas and told the local gardaí that somebody was peddling heroin in your street the perpetrators would be busted in no time. Which is how it should be. Which is how it wasn't in The Mun!

In an ideal world people would have the utmost respect for whichever law enforcement agency is responsible for reducing criminal activity and solving crime. In that same ideal world the law enforcers would respond to residents in distress; they would remove the problem, and the people would be able to get on with their lives. But not so in The Mun. In The Mun people were so disheartened by lack of official co-operation that they felt there was no other option than to deal with the problem themselves.

Anyone who lived in Ballymun at that time knew of furniture and electrical appliances being thrown over balconies, and one rumour tells of dealers themselves being evicted the quick way. And I suppose to anyone who has never had to live in that environment it must seem like a scene from an old Chicago gangster movie. But these people were nothing more than parents, angry parents who were sick to death of being bullied by the drug dealers, and were beyond any hope of getting any sort of legal intervention into their plight. The scenario was the same all over The Mun, as it was in other areas of the city.

Knowing that the guy next door is a drug dealer was not too difficult work out, particularly when you can hear his customers talking about their 'gear', and you see them injecting on the stairwell your children have to use when the lifts are broken. You go to the gardaí and tell them, with the backing of Concerned Parents Against Drugs, but nothing is done and the trading continues. As the trading continues so does the filth that addicts leave behind, and so the mounting fear and frustration of the parents trying to keep their children safe turns into anger; at the dealers, at the gardaí and at the housing authorities.

I am no vigilante; but under those circumstances, if no recognised authority were doing anything to help alleviate the situation, then yes, I would certainly resort to taking the law into my own hands, if that's what anyone wants to call the action taken by parents in The Mun. And would I be too particular about how their belongings left the flat? I suppose not.

Eventually the Corporation joined in with the craic, and sent notices of evictions to convicted drug dealers, proposing to them the same options as Concerned Parents Against Drugs: 'Clean up or get out'. Some cleaned up, some left of their own accord, some were evicted by the Corporation, and some dug in their heels, put bars on their doors, locks on their windows . . . and once again it was up to the parents of the kids of The Mun to rectify the situation.

* * *

Before I take this subject any further I need to point something out about myself. I am the most apolitical person I know of. I really couldn't care less which political party is in government. There was a time when I would have crawled over hot coals in order to vote. After all, women have died in the past to make it possible for women like me to make a difference when it came to voting time. I used my very important vote year after year. Never sticking to one party, but carefully selecting the candidates with the best manifestos, and the stronger politicians. And I can't believe how long it took for it to sink into my brain that no matter what manifestos said, no matter what politicians said, once they get into power the kudos seems to go to their heads and they do whatever they want anyway.

So what I have to say about Sinn Féin and its association with The Mun is in no way a reflection of my political affiliations. Nor is what I have to say any reflection on the political allegiances of the people of The Mun. Nor do I want to give the impression that The Mun is a hide-out for the IRA, or any other such nonsense anyone may think they are reading between the lines. For the purposes of what I have to say Sinn Féin is nothing more than another label. In this case they could be called The Daft Party, it doesn't matter, because what they did in The Mun was not always within the political framework as seen by the rest of society.

I am *very* aware of the connections that they say exist between Sinn Féin and The IRA. And perhaps those connections do exist. I don't know, and I am not prepared to speculate. I could have gone to the trouble of asking Sinn Féin politicians about how they felt when bombs went off in crowded streets and killed innocent people. I could even have asked them about such bombings that were attributed to the IRA. But, to the best of my knowledge no bombs ever went off in The Mun that could be attributed to the IRA, Sinn Féin or any other political party or extremist group. So for that kind of tale you need to read a different book. *Two Little Boys* by Edward O'Neill[1] would help you out with that kind of subject matter.

Realistically, the members of Sinn Féin who were actively working within The Mun over the years since it was built were probably after votes just like any other politicians. The difference is that they were active twenty-four/seven, three hundred and sixty-five days of the year. The difference is that they got up off their arses and did something when there *wasn't* an election due. They didn't just turn up and canvass wearing stupid rosettes when they needed votes; they stood alongside the people when the Corpo tried to

---

1. 'Two Little Boys: An Account of the Dublin and Monaghan Bombings and their Aftermath' (Currach Press, 2004).

evict tenants who were in arrears after the rent strike in the 70s. And when once again the people of The Mun had their backs against the wall by the drug dealers and the feckless gardaí, it was Sinn Féin who came out to help.

And apart from gossip, that's where the story ends.

Everyone in The Mun will tell you that Sinn Féin helped out when it came to evicting drug dealers out of the flats. Some will tell you they were heroes, some will tell you that they really were vigilantes. But nobody will put their name to their opinion. And yet, this 'no comment' atmosphere seems more to be one born out of respect rather than fear. Even those who tell you that Sinn Féin (or sometimes The 'Ra) went too far, but we were still glad to see the back of the dealers. To quote one nameless figure drinking a pint of Guinness in the Penthouse: 'The Ra went way too fucking far. Sure you couldn't even get a bit of draw at one time.'

A comment which, to the exponents of the school of 'One Drug Leads to Another', may be not such a bad thing. But to those who just liked a smoke to relax, it was a pain in the arse to have to go to Finglas or Glasnevin for a bit of pot. (You could buy pot in Glasnevin!) To the Sinn Féin politicians pot was a drug like any other, because Sinn Féin politicians are politicians like any other at the end of the day. To that end, there was no point in removing the weed without taking out the root.

Councillor Larry O'Toole is a Sinn Féin politician. It is also reported in the news that he is an anti-drugs activist in the Darndale area. But journalists have proved themselves to be so unworthy of belief time and time again that you have to wonder if they are not stretching a point here. I really cannot tell you if Larry is an anti-drugs activist, because he wouldn't tell me. (I smile when I recall *his* smile at the question.)

Larry could be anyone's cuddly, grey-haired grandfather. You would never see him in the street and think, 'Now there's a man to be scared of.' Actually, you would probably give him your seat on a bus; after all, he is getting on a bit. You certainly wouldn't think him the kind of man to get involved with the kind of activity that included swift furniture-removal over the balconies. Not that I am accusing him, or any member of Sinn Féin, of any such activity. That's just gossip, and we all know how harmful the wrong kind of gossip can be to people's reputations. No, whatever strife anyone may have had with Larry O'Toole or his son, Lar, I suspect it was likely to be of their own making. Perhaps their involvement in getting rid of drug dealers has, like the death of Mark Twain, been greatly exaggerated. Then again, perhaps their involvement in helping problem areas get rid of drug dealers has something to do with what happened at St Joseph's Church in Poppintree on 16 May 1996. It is a mystery that will probably remain so. I can only tell you what happened, and let you make up your own mind.

It was the morning of Laura O'Toole's first Holy Communion. I know that she was filled with the same excitement that any little girl feels on that special day, as she got ready to go to church with her family, including Larry O'Toole, her grandfather. Her father, Lar O'Toole, had been having problems with the guy who lived above him for some time. It was known locally that he had some involvement with drugs, but not in any big way. Peter McCann was the neighbour from Hell, and regularly taunted Lar and his family from the balcony above. And the morning of the First Holy Communion was no different. Peter McCann was throwing things down onto the balcony below and generally making a nuisance of himself, spoiling what was supposed to be a special day. So Larry Senior went upstairs to, 'have a word with him'. But Peter McCann had a metal grille in front of his door, and his only reply to Larry's request for peace for the sake of the child was to spit in the grandfather's face before shutting the door again.

So as to keep things as normal as possible for little Laura and her ten-year-old brother Gavin, who was due to be singing in the choir at Mass, the family set off for church and took their places in the pew. Larry sat with his son Lar to his right, and his wife and grandchildren to his left. The church was full of little children and their families, and it should have been one of the safest places on earth for the O'Toole family that day. Instead, it turned into the location of the biggest nightmare the family had ever been through. Larry didn't see Peter McCann enter the church, and even when he looked up when he heard the words: 'Larry O'Toole—You're dead!' he didn't realise instantly that the man wearing a peaked cap and dark sunglasses as he pointed a gun at him was his son's neighbour.

The gun went off, and what happened next, although over in a matter of moments, will run in slow motion in Larry O'Toole's memory for as long as he lives. The first bullet skimmed Lar's cheek, and in a flash Larry turned and threw himself across his wife and grandchildren in an attempt to protect them with no thought for his own life. He was a parent protecting his family, like any other man in that church would have done under the same circumstances. So Peter McCann fired again, shooting Larry in the back before making a run for it. And what should have been one little girl's happy time, turned into carnage, horror and disbelief.

Panic erupted in the church as people dived for cover, but not Lar O'Toole, he took off after the gunman in what was probably an instinctual reaction fuelled by rage. He caught up with Peter McCann outside, and grappled with him; but the gun went off and Lar was shot again, this time in the chest. Again the gunman made a break for it, but by this time the incensed parents were out of the church and had joined in with the chase. So too had the McDonnagh Traveller family who were camped by the side of the road near the church. McCann was overpowered by the parents and the Travellers, and probably would have sustained a lot more injuries than the fractured skull he received had the gardaí not happened by to break up the mêlée.

It doesn't take a lot of thought to imagine what the scene was like outside the church that day. Pandemonium broke out, and little children cried and clung to their parents and grandparents in fear while they waited for the ambulances to come for Larry, his son and Peter McCann.

Not little Gavin O'Toole though; little Gavin ran away. His poor little mind could not deal with what had just happened, with what was still happening, and so the adrenaline surging through his tiny body took his legs in flight to the middle of a nearby field. He sat in the middle of the field, his body wracking with sobs, his heart pounding with fear, his soul grieving for what he saw as the death of his loved ones. He screamed when anyone tried to get near him, and it was some time before he believed that his Da and his Granddad were alive, and although not well, were both going to live.

You see, that's the reality of the situation. For whatever reason Peter McCann got up the courage to walk into that church on that day above all others, with a gun in his hand that he was prepared to kill with . . . the outcome was the same severe emotional trauma that *any* family suffer when loved ones are hurt or killed, particularly when that attack is of such a violent nature.

What emotion possessed Peter McCann that day that enabled him to walk into that church in the first place? Fear, drug-induced confidence, anger, or perhaps something a little more sinister? Only Peter McCann can fully answer that question; But I doubt he ever will.

Of course gossip abounds about this incident. Some say that Peter McCann owed a large bill to the big drug barons who put the screws on him in a 'kill or be killed' scenario. Others say he *offered* to do it in order to pay off a drugs bill. Then again, there is the rumour that he was a nut case. But the question still remains: *Where did he get the gun*?

The trauma suffered by the O'Toole family that day is ongoing. Larry still has a bullet lodged in his body, Gavin and his sister have grown up living with the distress they cannot shake off to this day and I have no doubt that many of the children who were there that day feel the same.

* * *

No story of Ballymun would be complete without including the name Pat Tierney. Yes, I know he was a member of Sinn Féin, but let's leave his republican nature to one side and concentrate on the man himself.

Pat was born in Galway in 1957, the product of an out-of-wedlock pregnancy that was the epitome of scandals in those days. It is as unclear to me as it was to Pat as to whether or not his mother wanted to keep her baby; but for whatever reason, Pat ended up being brought up in religious institutions, and when he was only three years old his family abandoned him completely when they moved to live in England. Like so many others of the time, and like so many kids brought up by the nuns and the Christian brothers, Pat couldn't leave the country quick enough when it came time for him to stand on his own two feet.

Finding himself in Newfoundland in Canada and then in America, it seems as though Pat tried a different drug in every state, until eventually he was living in Wyoming where he was introduced to injecting with heroin, and ultimately he injected with a dirty needle. Perhaps in a kickback at the society that raised him Pat's life went from bad to worse, he went to England, in search of the family who had abandoned him at such an early age, but was deported back to Ireland after being found guilty of stealing a car stereo. It was while he was living in The Mun that Pat was diagnosed as being HIV positive in 1990. He blamed no-one but himself for the situation he found himself in; although he *did* question whether he would have contracted the disease had he been given a decent childhood. But then who wouldn't wonder about that in his position?

When he was first diagnosed he didn't worry so much about what was going to happen him, but whether or not his friends would still want to know him; whether he would still be welcome in their homes or be allowed to make contact with their children. Pat didn't need to be a rich man, but he *did* need his friends, without whom he couldn't see there being much point to life. But if he expected rejection from the people of The Mun because of his illness, he was very much mistaken in his thoughts.

Back in 1989 Pat had started teaching local children how to write poetry, particularly playground-style rhymes and soon The Rhymers' Club was established in Eamonn Ceannt Tower, where an average of sixty children would meet to learn all Pat could teach them about the poetry he loved so well. In August 1991, The Rhymers' Club was the recipient of The Ford Award for poetry from *The Evening Herald*, including £1,000, for their anthology of poetry *Spring Song*.

So, no, his friends *didn't* turn him away. His friends still trusted their children to his care. And his friends still admired and respected the man that Pat had turned out to be in spite of his upbringing, in spite of his drug addiction, and in spite of his illness. I doubt if the same situation would have been allowed in Howth.

But the people of The Mun are not ignorant. You cannot be ignorant and live in Ballymun. The ways of the world have no better training ground, and people make it their business to be fully aware of anything that may affect the well being of their families. Teaching children poetry, encouraging their education and bettering their lives is not a method of spreading the HIV or AIDS virus. The people who trusted Pat to take good care of their children's welfare knew that. So to his friends, the only problem was that *their* friend was seriously ill.

Pat Tierney was not only a character of The Mun, but also of the city, where he would read poetry in the street for passers-by on Grafton Street. He worked tirelessly to get rights for buskers in Dublin, and it was as a result of his efforts, which included chaining himself to the railings of St James' Hospital, that Dublin City Council stopped burying victims of AIDS in body bags, or 'bin liners' as Pat saw them. What were the authorities thinking of? What difference did it make to bury AIDS victims in coffins like anyone else? Once again, a Ballymunner had to fight bureaucrats in order to get them to see sense.

Pat didn't take medication for his illness. This was his own personal decision, and I have no idea why he went down the route he did. However, I suspect that he did not want drugs to interfere with his quality of life. Pat lived life to the full, and filled every moment with as much happiness he could glean from the world he lived in. Not the world of a junkie, for he had long since stopped injecting, but the world of the community that took him into their hearts as a shining example of how it was possible for *anyone* to change when they really wanted to. Pat didn't change his ways no matter where he travelled, not until he came to live in The Mun. Strange isn't it, how it took residency in a place that everyone considered so bad for Pat Tierney to really turn his life around?

That's not to say that Pat was ever a bad person, just that his life took him down a road that eventually took his life, but before that happened Pat turned his life around, made himself a home in The Mun, and will live on as a man who deserves to be remembered.

One night Pat left The Mun with his rucksack over his shoulder as usual. But this time the rucksack held something a bit different to the usual books and pens it usually held. Inside his bag Pat carried a rope, with which he intended to hang himself in the grounds of a convent in Drumcondra. He died on 4 January 1996, which comes so closely on the heels of New Year's Eve that I can't help wondering if all the 'Happy New Year' thing got to him a bit. Because Pat was ill by this stage, and it may well have been that he decided he wasn't going to have a happy year ahead, and if he couldn't be happy . . . what was the point to it all?

And that would be the end of a sad tale; were it not for the ensuing events, overseen by none other than Larry O'Toole.

Pat Tierney's body was taken to hospital where he was pronounced dead on arrival. Pat had wanted to die, he had not intended to be rescued, and so the pronouncement was accepted by his friends as what Pat would have wanted. There's no point in making a man live when he really doesn't want to.

But it was not Pat's way to go out quietly. The very place
that he chose to take his own life was selected as a final 'up
yours' from the man who was moved from institution to
institution all his childhood. If he could cause the church
some embarrassment by his carefully timed and placed
departure, then so be it. Of course Pat didn't tell me this; he
couldn't tell me or anyone else about why he chose that
particular location because this was something he needed to
do alone. I can only assume that his choice was *not* made out
of any need to die on holy ground.

There had been a scandal in 1993 at the same convent in
Drumcondra, when the Sisters of Charity exhumed the
bodies of over a hundred women who had died in that place.
Women who had worked their lives away in the laundries
and the gardens of the convent in much the same way as the
pregnant girls of St Patrick's had. The nuns wanted to sell
the land, which they did in receipt of one million pounds,
but only after the bodies had been removed and interred
elsewhere. Perhaps Pat saw this as the ultimate insult; one that
he returned to the nuns by taking his own life in that place.

His body was taken out to Ballymun, back to his flat on
the twelfth floor of Eamonn Ceannt Tower. Unfortunately,
when they carried his body into the tower they found that
the lifts were out of order, (surprise surprise!) and they had
one hell of a job getting Pat to the party. But get him there
they did. He was laid out on the balcony in the fresh winter
air while his friends carried out a wake in his honour that
went on for three to four days. Larry O'Toole doesn't
remember exactly how long—I wonder why?

Pat left a will; not that he was a rich man, just that he had
a few debts he needed to pay. That's how honest a man Pat
was. If he owed you a couple of quid, you got a mention in
the will. He owed a bit of back rent to the Corporation, and

this too was included in the list of debts to be paid following his death:

> ~~To Dublin Corporation; the rent I owe them. Fuck the Corporation!~~
> I guess there wasn't much respect in Pat's heart for the housing authority. But then respect always has to be earned.

I never knew Pat Tierney, but I have spoken to many people who knew him well. Apparently it wasn't difficult to know Pat; his life was the open book that eventually became his autobiography, *The Moon on my Back*. Unfortunately, I never got to read this book either, but I am sure it would make compelling reading. I am sorry I never knew him, because from what people have to say about him I know he enriched the lives of others in a way that so many people on this planet fail to do, mainly through their blindness to what living actually means. He didn't want adoration; he didn't want a fortune; Pat Tierney had got nearly all he wanted from life. He had friends, and he had the ability to pass on his wondrous talents to children who will never forget him as long as they live. And how many of us can say that? All he was lacking was his health, but even then, he bravely carried on until he could carry on no more.

Pat Tierney's life was bad before he arrived in Ballymun. But amongst the people of The Mun, he managed to turn his life around; to make his life into something worthwhile, something that gave hope to others in turn. While Ballymun was being looked down on by Dublin society in general, it provided the nourishment that Pat Tierney needed so badly: love, friendship and a reason to go on, for as long as he could. Rest in Peace, Pat.

Chapter 11
The Urban Cowboys

Horses have been part of Ireland's culture for hundreds of years. They once worked on the farms where they paid their own way handsomely with their labour before tractors made them all but redundant. They pulled Guinness wagons and omnibuses before the combustion engine took over. Irish racehorses, trainers and jockeys are famed worldwide for their exceptional skills, and their links with the Irish people are renowned across the globe. They towed the stalls into Moore Street market where they waited patiently while their owners sell their fruit and veg. They pulled the barges on the canals and, perhaps most famously of all the horses in Ireland, they pulled the myriad of caravans (so famed and romanticised around the world that there is now a roaring tourist trade in horse-drawn caravan holidays) belonging to the Travelling people, as they roamed the roads of Ireland.

Well, perhaps there was a time when the Travellers were the most famous association that there was between horses and Ireland. But that was in the days before the emergence of the Knights of Dublin, the urban cowboys who raced through the streets of Ballymun, Ballyfermot and Clondalkin night after night on horses that soon became as famous as the fillies that raced the tracks over the Epsom Downs.

The Travellers started to move into the outskirts of Ballymun in the early 1980s, setting up camp at the turn for Santry Lane, in the lay-bys in Poppintree and by the side of the road near Ballymun Library. And with them came the horses and ponies that aided survival in a world where 'the knackers' were still not welcome. Unless of course you needed a cheap spare part for your car, a used tyre, or a bit of advice as to what to do with a particularly taxing mechanical problem. The Travelling people were nothing if not experts in the workings of every engine ever built. Yet again, a necessary part of their lives. When you ran the risk of being evicted from a piece of land in the middle of the night it wasn't good to be hindered by a stalling engine. If your car wouldn't start in spite of being towed around the estate or with the help of heavy-duty jump leads you could take it to the knackers, and some ten-year-old kid would start it so quickly that it could leave a mechanically minded man with deep feelings of inadequacy.

It wasn't unusual to look out of the bedroom window in the morning to see piebald ponies munching away on the grass between the flats, grazing contentedly. Nor was it unusual to be entertained by ad-hoc cabarets as they (the gardaí) tried to round them up and the ponies deftly avoided capture by sidestepping their grasping hands in scenes reminiscent of a Laurel and Hardy sketch. Invariably, a van would turn up (or a smart estate car with English registration plates), a Traveller would come ambling over to the horses, and they would be led away meekly, leaving the gardaí looking thoroughly stupid, only to find their own way back to the lush green pastures of Ballymun again with a couple of days. The horses seemed to like the fertile grass that grew prolifically all over Ballymun and would happily munch away in between dodging the gardaí until their owners came to collect them.

Of course these horses were a source of attraction and entertainment to local children who had grown up without any of the local amenities once promised by Dublin Corporation. The horses would have been an attraction to kids *anywhere*, but these were kids who had no cinemas, ice rinks or bowling alleys as they had once been told they *would* have. Any entertainment for the children of The Mun was organised by the people, like the Summer Project that ran for many years. (There *was* the swimming pool, but they could hardly spend every day of the summer holidays there.) The knackers' horses were fairly tame, and didn't try to run away when the first adventurous children approached them. They were familiar with the company of children, so they didn't object when the kids climbed on board and rode around a bit. And any kid who rode around will tell you that it was the best fun ever. The gardaí or the Travellers turning up to round up the equine runaways only added to what was already an exciting adventure. To the kids of Ballymun, jockeying the horses took them off to the Wild West, where they became General Custer and Geronimo until they had to run away from the law or the Travellers, at which point *they* became the outlaws.

In the late 1980s someone on the estate bought a horse and brought it home to Ballymun. I have no idea who this person was, but I can well imagine the envy of his friends as he proudly paraded what would have been seen almost as a badge of manhood, for all to see. Of course, where one child has an interest, the other children will follow suit, and little by little more and more horses began to live in The Mun. In a town where kids generally had to make their own excitement, often dangerously so; horses fitted the bill in a way that a swimming pool could never have done. The feeling a teenage boy could get from riding a horse across the 'plains' with the wind whistling past his ears as he whispered words of encouragement to his steed could not be matched in any way by a couple of lengths of the pool and a bit of larking around. All thoughts of cinemas, bowling alleys and ice rinks were replaced by the time-consuming ownership of Shetland ponies, piebalds, greys, Palominos and any other kind of horse that was for sale, often for a boy's Confirmation money.

On the first Sunday of every month horses change hands at Smithfield market with a spit on the palm and a shake of a hand, and in the late 1980s many of these ponies ended up living on the grasslands of Ballymun. Up to 2,000 horses would be traded in the old cobblestone market between the Travellers and those seeking to be part of the urban cowboy legend. It was not only in Ballymun that kids were taking to the streets on their steeds; it was happening all over Dublin in epidemic proportions. But nowhere else had the vast open grasslands where the horses could graze and be raced without obstacles getting in the way. At first, little thought was given to provisions of niceties like saddles, tackle or stirrups. Papers rarely, if ever, exchanged hands, a spit on the palm before shaking hands being all that was needed to secure a deal before tying a rope around its neck and riding your horse home to be tethered to the railings outside the flats; just like a cowboy does before entering the saloon.

In many ways the advent of horses in Ballymun was a good thing. Kids who owned horses were far less likely to get involved with other pastimes like joyriding or drug taking. Getting chased by the cops in a stolen car was thrilling, but dangerous. Riding a horse across a field was thrilling and dangerous, but death or a prison sentence was a less likely outcome to the practice of galloping down Sillogue Road or across the fields of Poppintree. Similarly, riding a horse as fast as the wind was also a drug in itself, a drug that could not be matched by *anything* that could be injected intravenously.

Owning a pony was the start of a dream for many Ballymun kids. Ireland's heritage of breeding and training some of the finest racehorses in the world provided the aspiration for these kids to become the next Lester Piggott or Steve Cauthen. And it was a dream that was easy to believe in when your pony took first place in one of the races that took place in Ballymun.

The kids who took part in these races came from other areas such as Finglas, to challenge the Ballymun horses. Someone would hold out a jar, and everyone taking part in the race would put a tenner in, with the winner taking the whole pot. Kids who used to rush home from school to watch their favourite TV show or play on their Playstations until their brains melted would now dash home to take care of their horses out in the fresh air; grooming them, feeding them and training them to win. And of *course* parents approved of the new 'hobby' that was keeping their children away from the areas of danger that were becoming so prevalent in Ballymun. Well, most of the time.

Ann and John were sitting watching TV together one night on a rare occasion when every one of their children was out at the same time. But Ann's viewing pleasure was being disrupted by a noise she kept hearing outside. At fisrt she thought it was her neighbour doing something in the garden. Then she thought it could be a stray dog rummaging in the bin. And so she got up to chase off what she was sure was a little four-legged animal. But when she opened the back door it was a much larger four-legged animal she came face to face with, as an enormous horse poked its head through the door and neighed at her. So much for a quiet night in!

The horse swung its head in the direction of the sink, and Ann realised that the poor thing was thirsty. She ran to the hall (ever the animal lover) to get a bucket to give the creature some water, but when she dashed back into the kitchen the horse had made its way in through the back door, and was taking up most of the floor space in the kitchen. She wrestled to move the horse out of the way, fighting for supremacy over the sink region where the horse had worked out the water came from.

As she finally started to fill the bucket, the horse lurched forward and drank like it was dying of thirst. Which it may well have been had Ann not had the good sense and decency to realise that it needed water.

Ann's teenage daughter Emma was known as something of a horse whisperer around Ballymun. She had a natural talent with horses and was renowned for her calming influence over nervous or frightened ponies. Many of the horses that changed hands so casually in Smithfield Market were barely broken in, and many an arm, shoulder or head was bitten by a wild horse. Bones were not only broken during races; Temple Street Hospital also saw many cases where kids had been kicked or even stomped on by untrained horses.

But when Emma was around the horses behaved like angels with hooves. Hairy, currently working as a doorman at The Penthouse owned one of the biggest horses around. But not only was this horse huge, it also had the temperament of a Rottweiler with learning difficulties. (See, there are some areas where political correctness just doesn't work.) If there was one thing that this monster of a horse objected to by snorting, stamping its hooves and biting the heads of anyone close by, it was being put into a horse-box. And Hairy had the scars to prove it. So whenever Hairy needed to get the horse into his box to take it somewhere, he would call for Emma and she would lead it inside, gently whispering in its ear, without so much as a whinny from the horse from Hell.

But that was the nice side of it; that was the romantic version, like a scene from *Into the West*; boys and their ponies, racing one another across the fields of dreams where, if only for a short while, they became champion jockeys and heroes of the Wild West. But then there was also a darker side to the famed ownership of horses in Ballymun, a side to the story where some poor horses suffered dreadfully, mainly through ignorance.

These were kids who had been born and raised in Ballymun. The only time they saw animals other than cats, dogs or birds was on visits to the zoo or on TV. Although they *felt* it their heritage to own and race horses, they were not born into the equine environment that the Travellers lived in from birth. A ten-year-old child who has lived with horses all his life, whose family depends on the welfare of those horses, understands what it takes to look after a horse. A ten-year-old child on a housing estate, in the middle of a concrete jungle has no such innate knowledge. Learning how to look after a horse was something the kids learned gradually, like the fact that a horse needs to drink 8–10 gallons of water every day, just to function normally. And so it was inevitable that some horses died as a result of the neglect brought on by ignorance. When the vet had to be called out time and time again to shoot some poor kid's horse because it had been injured in a race, or had a disease of some sort, the Dublin Society for the Prevention of Cruelty to Animals began to get involved, and once again Ballymun was at war with the authorities.

From my home in a small country town, where the most exciting event of any one week is the local rugby match, it is easier for me to understand both sides of the coin here. Theresa Cunningham, Director of the DSPCA worked tirelessly to get the horses *out* of Ballymun only because she cares about the horses. The kids in Ballymun worked tirelessly to *keep* the horses in Ballymun, only because *they* cared about the horses.

The other difference between Holy St Theresa (as she was called by local kids; not in a respectful way, the title was bestowed out of nothing more that sarcasm) and the kids of Ballymun was that she had the backing of every relevant authority, up to and including the government. Theresa Cunningham, the DSPCA, the gardaí and the government all worked together to try to stop the kids from keeping the horses that they so cherished.

The parents of the kids with horses were furious. They had found a way to keep their children off the streets, away from crime and drugs. It was a way that worked, and would continue to work so long as there was some sort of co-operation from the government. But all that came was a draconian new horse law that was passed in 1996; it was a law that gave the authorities the power to remove the horses from the streets of Ballymun.

The new law said that you had to be over sixteen to own a horse; any parent who had a child *under* 16 with a horse was automatically the new owner of the animal. To own a horse you now also needed to own an acre of land; something that was impossible when you lived in a high-rise block of flats.

But for the horse to be licensed these criteria had to be covered. The government was very aware that most of the urban cowboys could not comply with the new law, and it moved swiftly to implement the new rulings. But while doing so, they broke the hearts of Ballymun kids.

Taking away a boy's horse was not like taking away his skateboard or his Playstation. Boys and girls, who loved them dearly, owned most of the horses that were tethered up outside the flats at nighttime. They were friends as well as steeds. These horses took up so much of their riders' lives that to have them taken away was like losing everything that made life worthwhile. The horses, a mismatch of every horse you can think of from Shetland ponies to shire horses, were flesh and blood; real living creatures that needed a lot of care and attention, and the children devoted every waking hour to their needs. The horses of The Mun were no passing fad and there was nothing that could supersede or replace them.

I can see why the authorities were concerned about the night racing, and the way in which some of the horses were kept. And I feel a lot of grief for the horses that suffered at the hands of some ignorant children. But this isn't about the government, or how they feel. This is about Ballymun, and how many times the people of that estate felt kicked in the teeth by the authorities they tried so hard to reason with over the years. They had found a way to live a dream, and would it really have hurt to help them to *live* the dream, rather than *outlaw* it? I don't know how much money it cost the authorities in their battle against the urban cowboys from when they first got involved with the situation in the mid 1980s through the passing of the new law up to present day. I don't know how much it has cost the authorities in total to then keep these horses at pounds when they are rounded up in the middle of the night. But it doesn't take a genius to work out that co-operation with the owners of the horses, provisions of stables and instruction etc, would not have cost nearly as much to the Irish taxpayer as the route the authorities have taken for the past twenty years.

It's easy for me to sit here now, an adult, and see all that was wrong with the idea of keeping ponies tethered outside concrete flats. But such understanding does not come easy to a 13-year-old boy who wakes up to find that the pony he has lovingly cared for, practically lived with for over two years, has been spirited away in the night during a secret police round-up. And so it was bound to be that the parents of these distraught youngsters felt anger in their hearts towards callousness of the authorities that had hurt their children so much. Anyone who has ever had to have their precious pets put to sleep will know the anguish that these children went through on losing their beloved horses. The sadness we all feel on losing an animal by having it put to sleep is so huge, words cannot do the feeling any justice. I cannot bear to think how much worse that feeling would be if our pets just disappeared into the night, to be taken to some alien place.

All over Ballymun children cried themselves to sleep over the loss of their beloved companions. Every day more kids went to school with long faces without having been able to say good morning to their equine friends. Some kids didn't even bother going to school. What was the point? It seemed as though no matter what you tried to do to better your life, to better the lives of the children, somebody in authority would always be there to put a stop to it, take away your dreams and put you right back in your place. From the days of the CBs to the days of the Urban Cowboys, the gardaí were ever present to say, 'No, you can't do that!' Kids who used to spend all their time with their ponies now hung around the sheds like they did in the old days. And, although I have no evidence to support the theory, I am sure it has to be so that more than one kid ended up on drugs he would never have touched had he still got his horse to take care of.

Kids began to sleep out in the open with their horses, to protect them from becoming prisoners of war in the battle that (in their minds) the other side had started. More than one horse found itself 'stabled' in flats, houses, garages and garden sheds as kids did all they could to hide their precious companions. Some parents simply could not bear the grief that they watched their children go through day after day. The hurt of their little ones became just a bit too much for some parents to take, and so they took the law into their own hands. The horses that were rounded up in Ballymun in the dead of night were taken to horse pounds in Cork, where they were imprisoned behind high walls, as far away from the open grasslands they knew as the authorities could get them. So, some local men set off for Cork, in an attempt to liberate the horses that had been 'stolen' from their children. But when they got there they found the compound security to be tighter than that of Mountjoy and Ballymun Garda station put together. They ended up falling into a bog, and getting back to their vehicles soaked to the skin and abandoned their 'mission'.

A group of resourceful parents got together to help their children show the authorities that they really *did* care for their horses, and that they were very serious about looking after their welfare. A workingmen's club had been built on the outside of the estate, but had been abandoned as an unfinished project when a drinks licence had been refused (the owner of the Towers having put in an objection), and it was there that the Ballymun Horse Association first began to fight back at the authorities in an organised, carefully planned way. The old club became stables for around twenty horses that were fed, watered and groomed as well as horses in any fancy stable. While the children went to school, which was often a parental condition of owning a pony, the unemployed parents of the kids would watch over the stables.

It was a situation the guards were uneasy with. They would drive past the stables and watch, but they knew full well that to do anything about the situation in broad daylight would have led to a full-scale riot. And as night fell they could do little more than watch again as the races continued in the fields on the back roads that led to the airport. It was not the way of the Ballymun gardaí to create a situation that could be avoided. Better for them to wait until everyone was asleep while they helped the men from the pounds round up the horses and ponies and take them away.

To get a horse back from the pound was, (or should I say is, as the roundups are still going on to this day) no easy task. Just like when a car is towed away there is a daily charge for 'storage'. And in the case of a horse that charge is €168 for the first day and €25 for every day thereafter. Of course, bearing in mind that it can take days to find out which pound a horse has been taken to; this charge is rarely for one day only. Some kids who have reared their horses from foals simply cannot get the money together to get their horse back from the pound. So, from there they are usually 'fostered' out to people who have other horses. At least, that's what the kids believe. However, the Control of Horses act makes it very clear that horses not claimed after five days will be disposed of 'at the authorities' discretion', which I find a bit sinister. Before the owner of the horse can take his or her beloved friend home not only has the 'fine' to be paid but they also have to fill out an affidavit to say that they will comply with the conditions of keeping a horse as set out in the Control of Horses Act. When a horse is bailed out of the pound the authorities take €25 as the charge for a horse licence. However, nobody ever actually receives the licence they have paid for, because to do so the conditions have to be complied with; and as one of those main conditions is that each horse must have one acre of land to itself, no horse owner in Ballymun ever received the piece of paper they needed.

Eventually, the government felt it had to do something more in order to bring the situation under better control. It was obvious that the Control of Horses Act of 1996 had only inflamed passion in the horse owners and in their parents, and that real co-operation was needed if there were ever to be any sort of progress towards a better understanding in all parties involved. But nothing happened overnight. The government is notoriously long-winded and meeting after meeting followed protest after protest, and it was to be many years before the government finally came to realise that the only *real* way to control the situation with the horses was to finance stable and equestrian centres, and to involve the Garda Equestrian Department in an effort to build bridges across the huge gap that had developed between the Ballymun people and any form of authority. At the time of writing, the Ballymun Horse Association is awaiting the €2.5 million that the government has promised them for new stables. The kids are excited about the prospect of not worrying about their charges being taken away in the night any more. However, it is a rather strange agreement that has been come to. The government are giving the Ballymun Horse Association a plot of land on which to build their new stables. This plot of land is seven acres in total. The stables are to house thirty horses. Now, I know I left school at thirteen, and maths has never been my strong point, but in order to comply with their own law, should the government not be giving the thirty horses thirty acres of land? Isn't that just a *classic* example of the kind of back-pedalling that made me lose faith in politicians in the first place.

Of course, if they had only had the sense to realise this in the first place, a lot of time, money, resources and heartbreak could have been avoided.

Tony McElligot, his wife Victoria and the late Kathleen Maher should be given some sort of community award in recognition for the work they have done to help the kids of Ballymun keep their horses. Tony is an unassuming man who takes no credit for the stables in The Mun, quickly passing any such credit offered on to his wife and her late friend. It was Victoria and Kathleen who set up the stables in the first place, and it was these two mothers who fought the authorities all the way. However, without Tony the children would struggle for the help they need. Their respect for the man who does so much for them is the kind of respect that politicians only ever dream of.

Tony receives no financial rewards for the work he puts in to maintaining the concrete-block-built stables. But then, what kind of financial reward could make a man feel any happier than Tony feels as he watches the results of his work mould these kids into the kind of citizens any country would be proud of. When Tony has a horse in foal he doesn't think of how much money he can get for the newborn horse, but which kid at the stables should receive their own horse to look after. It is not only children who *own* horses who help out at the stables; many kids help out just for the love of it all. There *are* conditions to receiving a foal from

Tony free gratis; and the main condition is that you don't sell a horse he gives you. Someone did that once, and it really pissed Tony off. That really was looking a gift horse in the mouth, and as everybody knows, it's not right to do that. I know there are many other parents who help out too, and I am not dismissing their part in all of this, but Tony, Victoria and Kathleen are such wonderful examples of parenthood, of community spirit and of kicking back at the government that without them I am not sure the stables would exist at all now.

In 1999 a book called *Christy's Dream* was published. It is not a big book, less than thirty pages long, but the illustrations tell as big a story as the words, if you read it properly. Unfortunately Hampshire County Council *didn't* read it properly, and so this book ended up being used in a literary class that was discussing the travelling people of Ireland. The lesson plan asks children to imagine what it would be like to live where Christy lives, to compare the differences between Christy's and their own lives. It states that Christy's family were 'housed Travellers' of Ballymun, as apparently are most people who live on the estate. Now, I know I once lived in a caravan, but it never *went* anywhere!

Christy's dream is about a young boy who wants his own horse. Not at any stage of the story are Travellers mentioned. Not on any of the pages is it even *remotely* intimated that Christy's family are settled Travellers, or that Ballymun is a place where those tired of roaming are housed. So just where did Hampshire County Council education offices derive this piece of information from? Well, according to them it is '. . . evident from the pictures that he is a housed Irish Traveller.' To me this is just another example of people living in their ivory towers looking down on the 'deprived' people of places like Ballymun. Deprived, I don't think so. The people of The Mun may have been deprived the contemporary amenities that the Corpo failed to deliver, but nobody in their right mind could visit that stable and come away thinking that those kids didn't have 'it all'. I have written to Hampshire County Council to inform them how their assumptions (what a classic example of to *ass-u-me*) are way off track but they have not replied; I wonder why.

You only have to meet the child, now a man with a child of his own, on whom the book *Christy's Dream* was based, to know that John is not a Traveller, nor is his gorgeous little boy Darragh, nor are his parents (Victoria and Tony). Perhaps the McElligot family are not what middle class society deem as 'normal'. But perhaps the McElligot family don't see middle-class life as 'normal' either.

I am not suggesting that hoards of tourists turn up to visit the stables; not unless they are willing to make a financial donation anyway. But to visit those stables; to watch those kids with their horses; to hear the truth of the matter from their own mouths. That is one humbling experience. The stables have had many visitors that would read like the invitation list to a VIP party. The Foo Fighters, Jules Holland and Bono have all been there; and the site was also used for a modelling shoot. But the kids were so 'impressed' by their big-shot visitors that one of them had to make a phonecall to find out who the visiting band were because nobody there that night could remember what they were called. Sorry, Foo Fighters, but you really didn't make that big an impression, the kids are far too busy taking care of their horses to have their heads in the clouds over things that are so unimportant to them that . . . well, they forgot who you were!

When there is no room for the horses inside the block-built stables, the alternative are the well ventilated shipping containers that line the perimeter of the land the Ballymun Horse Association is currently squatting on. Vandals set one of these containers on fire one night. But before they set light to it they removed the horses, which were found peacefully grazing in an adjacent field the following morning. Even mindless vandals respect the work that is going on at the stables in The Mun.

Looking after horses is not a part-time job; a horse requires a lot more work than a dog or a cat would need. Changing a litter tray is nothing in comparison to mucking out a stable, and doesn't take nearly as long. Teaching a dog to sit and stay is a far cry from teaching a stallion how to trot. And as for learning to ride . . . what other four-legged friend could put a child through so much physical pain? And yet they are there, in their Reebok and Nike gear, their school uniforms that they hadn't the patience to change out of, and the obligatory green wellies; essential footwear in any stable.

But they don't care about the hard work, or the pain of the aching muscles when they go home at night. It's all part of looking after the horses; they know this, so they don't moan about it, they just get on with it. (When they fit in their homework is anyone's guess; but as all these children seem bright, I am sure they cope.) When Tony turns up in a forty-foot articulated truck the kids don't need to ask what they have to do. They spring into action, unlocking the back doors of the trailer so that a couple of lads can climb inside and start passing down enormous sacks of wood shavings (horse bedding) to the waiting hands and shoulders below. Puffing and panting, the kids pile the sacks together before sweeping out the inside of the truck. A huge tarpaulin is thrown over the sacks to protect the bedding from any rain that may come during the night, and is weighted down with wooden pallets so that the wind can't damage it either.

But the best sight of all in that Stables the day I visited was the one-day-old foal that her owner, a lovely, bright girl, was beaming with pride over. With its little, spindly legs slipping and sliding all over the place it followed slowly as two lads gently coaxed mummy out of her stall, all the time assuring her that baby was right there behind her, and was in very safe hands, those safe hands that surrounded the little foal as she followed her mother outside for the first time. They were the same safe hands that steadied the new life when the foal stumbled, but was never allowed to fall, as she was taken outside and introduced to her new home to the backdrop of a setting sun that was almost a poetic vision. If there is a stable anywhere in the world where that foal could have been in safer hands; I don't know where it is.

Humble? No, humble doesn't really cover the feeling that place gives. In this rat race of a world too many people work with nothing but money and glory in mind. The things people believe they have to strive for in this world; big houses, cars and foreign holidays, pale into insignificance as you watch the unwavering dedication of the kids at the stables. No money could buy what these kids have. This isn't about money; this is about love, hard work and sheer bloody-minded determination. It is the kind of determination that could make countries great, if only governments would listen to what people really need.

I am sure David and Victoria Beckham's children have great fun in their luxury Wendy house that would be big enough for a whole family to live in; so huge that it had to have retrospective planning permission when their local Council received objections. But I am equally as sure that they have never known, and probably never *will* know, the satisfying happiness that the children in The Mun feel as they care for their horses. This is no passing phase; every day of every year these kids turn up for work, with no reward whatsoever other than the sheer joy of being with the animals they love so much.

They don't race any more. That's not what it's about. They don't have aspirations of becoming champion jockeys or world famous trainers. One lad wants to be a mechanic! What they *do* have is love, so much of it that it shines from them. Their pride in what they are doing is obvious, and they positively glow with it.

Chapter 12
Regeneration

Regeneration—is this really a word that can describe what Dublin City Council are doing in Ballymun at this present time? And if so, doesn't the actual definition of the word worry some people a little? It does me that's for sure. Regeneration of *anything* means to build again, to bring back what once was. Regeneration does *not* mean to scrap and start from scratch, diversifying into something different and better. And who is to say that the so-called regeneration of The Mun is going to be different and better? Dublin City Council, that's who. Formerly known as Dublin Corporation, the people who got it all wrong in the first place.

Apparently calling the new building 'apartments' instead of 'flats' makes some sort of difference in somebody's mind. (And that 'somebody' is no doubt employed by Dublin City Council's planning department.) Is the word 'apartment' supposed to sound posh or something? If the Council think that the people of Ballymun are so thick, so uneducated, so blind to what is going on around them that they can be fooled by psychological trickery; think again guys, because it's not working.

Going to a private school does not make for intelligence. Wearing a straw hat and blazer does not make a child any smarter than one who goes to school with a hooded top over their pristine uniform. Living in a detached house does not make anyone any cleverer than someone who lives in a concrete box or a bed-sit. And the people of The Mun are not stupid! They can see what the Council are doing, and in the main they are not happy about it.

My niece lives in one of the new 'apartments' that are being built all over The Mun. And on the face of it, she is one of the lucky ones. Her apartment is modern, fitted with the best of everything, including a wall of tinted glass that gives her a panoramic view of the cranes, the building sites and the heavy traffic. There are intercom systems fitted to the outside of the building, and nobody can get inside without being buzzed in by one of the tenants.

Well, that's how it *was* when she first went to live there with her baby son. But it has been some eighteen months now since the buzzers have worked. So to let visitors in the tenants have to go down in the lift and physically open the main door. How does this work when you have small children? I guess it means you have to take the children down in the lift with you while you open the door. And how pissed off would you be if you found a Mormon or a bible salesman standing there when you opened that door? They are only part way through building the place again, and already the tenants are suffering from the neglect of their landlords. But the authorities that be think they have been smart about it this time; you see, the apartment block that my niece lives in has been sold to private investors, and it is these private investors who are now responsible for the general upkeep of the building. In the couple of years since the apartments were built, nobody has ever come to clean the outside of the windows. It is an impossibility for tenants to do this themselves, and no matter how many times they clean the insides of their windows, they always look dirty because the outsides have just been ignored by the landlords.

When the first tenants moved into the apartments they had no idea what the ground-floor section of the building was going to become in the future. They expected shops, perhaps a nursery and some offices. But what they didn't reckon on was the Spar shop, the Chinese takeaway that stays open until 2am every night, or the nightclub, that is bound to attract drunks and drug users. Once again putting families into the same situation they were in before the 'regeneration'.

Just across from my niece's apartment is a brand new office block, built in the same style as the apartments, with dark-tinted windows. I would hate to see the bill for the smoked glass alone. And then, of course, there was the bill for replacing the glass when every window was smashed by kids with nothing better to do. And then there was the bill for replacing the glass that was replaced when it was broken by kids who had nothing better to do. Now, you would think that at this stage somebody would get it into their heads that perhaps leaving empty buildings with walls of 'targets' might not be the brightest of ideas, but no, as soon as the glass was broken again, out they came and replaced it again. And just who is picking up the bill for this stupidity? Let's not bother asking, because we all know that nobody would ever admit final responsibility for anything that ever happens in The Mun. As ever, the buck gets passed around, and the people get frustrated.

Some Ballymunners really have been quite lucky in that they are the new tenants of the houses that are being built all over the estate. But why couldn't they have built houses that *look* like houses? OK, they have walls, roofs and gardens, but they don't look much like traditional houses, the kind of homes the people of Ballymun have hankered over for years. If you built one of these houses on Griffith Avenue it would look downright peculiar. The Dublin City Council blurb about these houses declares them to be '. . . architecturally designed . . .'. As against houses designed by . . . butchers? Shoe salesmen? Software engineers? All houses are architecturally designed!

Everything being built in The Mun is ultra-modern; just as it was when the estate was initially dreamed up in someone's head in the 1960s. But modern designs are only ever applicable to a certain period in time, and very few modern designs manage to make it into the 'classic' category. Eventually modern architecture becomes a blip on the landscape, just like the flats became before they decided to regenerate. Of course, nothing in this life is perfect; certainly not Dublin City Council, and so no planning has been put into doing anything to update the two-storey houses that are not being demolished. Sillogue, Coultry, Shangan and Sandyhill Gardens will not be touched, but built around and ignored. OK, many of these houses are now privately owned, and no longer the responsibility of the Council; but wouldn't it be nice for the owners of these houses to have them spruced up? It wouldn't take a lot to make them look new again; certainly not as much as it keeps costing to replace the glass in the new office blocks. And is it really fair to make these people feel left out?

The council are doing the right thing (did I just say that?) by taking families out of tower blocks and giving them houses on the ground where their children can play safely in the sunshine. But they are ignoring the people of Ballymun who were once looked at as the privileged; the

families who live in the houses that were built in the 1960s.
These houses are tired now, and many are badly in need of
renovation, but as far as Dublin City Council are concerned, they may as well not exist. Would it really break the
bank to do them up a bit; to tidy up the communal grassed
areas? Probably not, but they are not planning on doing it
anyway.

They are planning to pull down the Penthouse to make
way for a car park. Of course it is always a good thing when
a damp, crumbling building is demolished to make way for
something new. But in the case of the Penthouse there is
nothing structurally wrong with the place. The logic behind
demolishing it to make way for a car park, only to have to
rebuild the pub again at another location is reasoning that
evades my understanding.

Larry was behind the bar when I first started drinking at
the Penthouse, and he still works there to this day; flying
around behind the bar in the lounge like a man a quarter
of his age. Larry forgets nobody. He remembers all his
regulars and doesn't need to be told what the drink to be
served is when the customer at the bar raises his finger in
an unspoken gesture. He recalls the old days when upstairs
was the best cabaret lounge around for miles, and yes, he
remembers the partygoers doing their Skippy imper-
sonations. He remembers Dr Blood, once manager of the
Penthouse. There were several explanations for this title,
one being that he was forever getting blood on his white
shirts while breaking up fights, and so had to keep a row of
shirts in his office. But I prefer the explanation that he
actually *looked* like a figure out of an old Hammer Horror
movie; or again, was that just me? (*When I told my son, on*
MSN *messenger, that they were knocking down the Penthouse,*
he went off to make a 'FUCK OFF!!!' *banner.*)

Now call me stupid, because when it comes to maths I really don't get the craic, but I don't think it takes a chartered accountant to work out that it is going to cost a whole heap more money to knock the pub down and rebuild it again on another location than it would to leave it where it is and go build a car park on one of the many open spaces around Ballymun? I mean, what's going to change? They will have the same customers, the same staff, the same craic, but the surroundings will not be as comfortable as the Penter; nor so familiar. The new pub may have carpets, fancy toilets and all the latest technology behind the bar, but how long is it going to take before the new place is as homely as the Penthouse came to be once the newness wore off? There used to be carpets in the Penthouse, but then somebody saw the nonsense of the cleaning bills and the floors were sensibly replaced by wood, just like so many of us have done in our homes.

Perhaps I write through nostalgic eyes. Perhaps if I were still living in Ballymun now, I would want rid of the Penter to make way for a new car park. Perhaps I would relish the prospect of going to a new and exciting pub for a night out. Then again, perhaps I would cry when the demolition squad move in to remove the physical evidence of so many of my memories. I don't know, I won't be there to see it happen, all I know is that it feels a bit odd to know that yet another part of my past is going to become rubble and dust. And I know that there are going to be many people who will feel very saddened by the loss of such an enormous part of their lives. So that said, no I do not think that it is wholly nostalgia that makes me feel sad that they are knocking down the Penthouse. It's a stupid waste of money. And once again, refurbishment, to bring it up to the standards of the proposed new pub, would cost far less to the Irish taxpayer that the plans as they stand at present.

And talking of stupid wastes of money, what was the craic with sandblasting and painting up the flats before they were demolished. You know, I am sure Dublin Corporation and Dublin City Council are chiefly responsible for the Irish jokes that circulate around the globe. When you take into account how many laughable things they have done, or not done, the ante-demolition clean-up of the flats has to be the icing on the cake.

From the first rumours that told of the flats being demolished to make way for houses on the ground gossip abounded about how it was all going to happen. And there was a story going around about the towers being taken apart segment by segment before being shipped to war-torn Bosnia and Croatia as emergency housing for refugees. (See, one man's muck and all that.) That kind of tied in with them cleaning up the outside of the flats first. (Although, I can't help thinking that the more economical solution would have been to power wash each segment *after* it was taken down, thereby eliminating the need for all the expensive hydraulic equipment needed to perform the cleaning operation while the flats were still in place.) Perhaps this rumour had some truth to it. But as we all now know, the Eastern-bloc countries are all doing fine now, with a roaring tourist trade, so they certainly wouldn't want Ballymun's cast-off flats ruining the picturesque landscapes, not even for free.

So when all came to all, the reasoning behind the hugely expensive clean up operation on the Ballymun flats amounted to nothing more than 'clean rubble' as someone aptly put it in the forum of the website *www.newballymun.com*. And they accuse the kids of Ballymun of being on drugs; I reckon someone at Dublin City Council needs to put the lid on the Prozac bottle.

There are grand plans to divide Ballymun into separate communities. This planning has been carried out thinking that if you put a load of people together in one place, give them a community centre and a row of shops, they will become a community. Has nobody in the planning department of Dublin City Council ever heard of the problems that separatism can cause? Not all separatism is about religion. Not all of the kids in Ballymun attend the stables every day. There *is* still an element that would rather pass their time smashing windows. And, just as it is in any town in any part of the world, Ballymun also has its gang culture and it's drug dealers, in spite of, or perhaps because of, the authorities who try to keep it all under control. It doesn't take a lot of imagination to see how the development of gangs from separate areas could cause trouble for the proposed communities. All little boys are members of a gang at some time of their lives; and most little boys keep that facet to their personality, no matter how old they get. As long as there are teenagers there will be gangs, there will be drugs, and unfortunately there is also likely to be trouble. Adding to the problems that teenagers can be with the element of separatism is just asking for trouble in my opinion.

I so hope I am not being pessimistic here. I wish nothing but the best for the people of Ballymun. They are lovely people, and deserve to be happy and content; not pushed from pillar to post by authorities who haven't got the vaguest notion what it's like to live there, and who refuse to listen when the people tell them what they *need*. Listening to the news reports about the first people moving into their new homes in Shangan Crescent was heart-lifting; but I worried a bit when Bertie Ahern stated that the idea was to take the estate back to what it was in the 1960s, when everything was clean and new. Well, here's a bit of news for you, Bertie, things have changed since then, and unless you have allowed for the social and economic developments that have taken place since the middle of the last century, things may start to go wrong again. I so hope that that the little girl who spoke on the news report about how wonderful her new home was still feels the same way in ten years' time. Listening to her awestruck voice as she announced the new house to be 'gorgeous' she so sounded like I felt when I moved into Sean MacDermott tower over thirty years ago.

There are people all over Dublin sitting in nice comfortable living rooms, in nice comfortable houses, in nice comfortable areas who have not only never even *been* to Ballymun themselves let alone live there, nor do they know a single person who has stepped foot on the estate, unless they have friends who work for Dublin City Council. Difficult as that is to comprehend when you take into account how many hundreds of thousands of people have lived there over the years; it is true nonetheless. These are people who wouldn't dream of having anything to do with The Mun because they *know* what the estate is like. Or at least they think they do! Intelligent, respectable people all over Dublin have come to believe the media reports about The Mun, and have come to the conclusion that the people who live there are a lower class of people than in places like Foxrock and Dalkey.

From a distance (a distance that can be as close as a shortcut through into Santry from Shangan Road) Ballymun is still seen as somewhere nobody wants to live; even though there are very expensive houses and apartments for sale there now. And in spite of the lowest price tag for the smallest apartment being €180,000, these properties are selling. Why are they selling in an area that became the first no-go area for Dublin Bus? They are selling because some people actually have the sense to realise that Ballymun is not what the media make it out to be. Not at its grass roots. The retail and workshop premises have been filled, and on the surface it looks as though things are going well.

However, if you *do* buy one of the new properties in Poppintree, and you also happen to have teenage children who may walk home through Ballymun from time to time, they are as likely to be stopped and have their pockets turned out as any other teenager in The Mun. The Ballymun gardaí are not going to give a damn whether or not your kids live in a house where the mortgage is paid on time every month. All they see are teenagers walking through Ballymun, and in their little heads teenagers = drugs in The Mun. Or perhaps that is being unfair; perhaps the gardaí are only aware that drugs are available anywhere.

Which takes me back to the authorities' lack of understanding when the people of Ballymun tell them what they *need* in order to be accepted as the decent part of the Dublin community that they actually are. They don't want to be seen as scroungers on the state; they want jobs, they want careers, they want decent standards of education for their children, from teachers who give a damn. And according to any statistics (see my earlier reference to Mark Twain) the number-one priority on any out-of-work-Ballymunner 'wish list' is full-time, properly paid employment. From this beginning they see a future where they can buy their own house and their one trip into town every week is for a night out, not to sign on. It's called independence, it's called having a decent standard of living, it's called making your own way in the world. So you can imagine the buzz of excitement when the building projects were announced; so many jobs for so many men, and right on their doorstep. Oh, if only that had been the case.

Yes there are Irish companies involved in the 'regeneration' of The Mun. And yes there are some men from Ballymun employed by these companies. But then there are also companies from England and as far away as Turkey completing contracts that ensures plenty of Irish money is sent back to the Turkish families whose menfolk have travelled so far to work. Or at least that's what the people of The Mun thought when GAMA moved into Ballymun, bringing with them their own workforce who, in the main, didn't speak a word of English, and had no idea that they were being badly mistreated until they started to talk to locals in broken English. The Turkish labourers soon began to realise that what was happening to them was not only morally wrong, but that their employers, GAMA, were breaking the law. Irish law.

Men who were brought over from Turkey to work on the regeneration of The Mun were told they would receive high wages and accommodation. What they got in reality was wages well below the legal floor and the promised accommodation translated into being herded into sheds at night, locked in. Some prisoners of war are treated to better living space than these men were expected to accept. In order to comply with employment laws in Ireland the men should have been paid a minimum of €7.99 per hour. But some Turkish men were getting a mere €2.20. Language barriers aside, it didn't take long for the Turks to realise that there was a huge shortfall in their wages, which was exacerbated by GAMA's deductions for accommodation. And it didn't take much longer after that for it to come to the attention of the government, who immediately took steps to rectify the situation.

GAMA's Irish solicitor, Richard Grogan, went on record as saying that everything was in order as far as the audit of GAMA's books were concerned. But he later back-tracked, and said that perhaps some workers had been underpaid by as much as 8%. Here we go on the maths again. The difference between €7.99 and €2.20 is €5.79. 8% of €7.99 is around 64 cent; somebody is telling porkies here! (Yes, I did work that out for myself.) However, as he then went on to say that, 'Somewhere in the region of twenty-nine folders have been delivered to the government . . .' It makes me wonder if the man actually has any ability to do sums at all.

The government of Ireland was, understandably, furious. I don't know why they felt it necessary to employ a Turkish company in the first place with so many unemployed in Ballymun already, but they did. And part of the arrangement was that workers coming over from Turkey to work on GAMA's sites would receive work permits. But once the investigation was under way work stopped on GAMA's sites, which also meant that wages, what little there were for the Turkish workers, stopped too. The outraged government also withdrew all the work permits that were given to GAMA's migrant workers, which meant that they could no longer work even if they wanted to.

It came to light that GAMA had opened bank accounts in Holland for the men, and this was where the surplus of the cash had been going. However, although GAMA tried to say otherwise, the Turkish men had no idea that these accounts existed until Irish government intervention uncovered them.

It was a mess; it is a mess, but hopefully it will all be worked out and the Turkish men will be reimbursed for the short fall in wages to the satisfaction of all parties. Well, apart from the men who watch from their windows and balconies as foreign nationals work from dawn to dusk on building sites where they feel they should be employed.

Of course it was not only GAMA who has been found guilty of exploiting the migrant workforce. There was also the case of the asylum-seekers employed by farmers for €1 or €2 an hour, being herded into cattle sheds at night and being fed on brown sauce and bread. There was the story of the Filipina woman employed as a beautician by Irish Ferries until RTE News got wind of her €1-an-hour wage. When they asked questions, she was sacked, but she refused to leave the ship, and so went backwards and forwards across the Irish Sea as media interest grew. Of course, as is the media's way, they eventually lost interest. A Turkish building company, a very large ferry company, and a lot of well-heeled farmers were breaking the law in this terrible way. Yet while the main of this exploitation was going on in The Mun, once again it had nothing whatsoever to do with the morals of the people of the estate.

One aspect of the new Ballymun that the planners seem to have got right is the opening of the Axis Centre in the early stages of the regeneration project. With a theatre, workshops, recording studios, rehearsal rooms for local bands, a crèche, restaurant and every other facility local community groups could need, they have at least covered some of the entertainment short fallings of 'old' Ballymun. With people like Victoria McElligot involved, I think it has a chance of survival.

We can only watch and wait now (and perhaps throw in a prayer) to see if Dublin City Council's grand designs are going to be the making of The Mun. By the year 2010 there will be nothing left (other than a few houses) to identify Ballymun Newtown as The Mun as it was. I for one hope it all works; that The Mun thrives under the nourishment of the people; that they are not given a hard time by the media; and that The Mun goes on to be recognised as the outstanding community it really is.

The Mun is full of proud, good people who have been made to feel like less-than-second-class citizens for far too long. And I hope that somewhere in the pages of this book I have managed to get that across to those who have failed to understand why people ended up living there, and why they had to fight for the simplest of rights that are so readily afforded to more affluent areas of the city.

I don't live in The Mun anymore, nor was I born there. But until my dying day I will be a Ballymunner. The Mun made me who I am today; it gave me the tenacity to fight back when I need to; it gave me the strength to walk away when I have to; and it gave me the ability to stand up and say so, when I see injustice taking place.

I am proud to say I came from Ballymun!

Ad hoc Tales

It was Saturday afternoon, and Jimmy was gumming (longing) for a pint. But, unfortunately, Jimmy had no money. However, what he *did* have was a huge chunk of cheese, several pounds in weight. He went into the Penthouse with the cheese under his coat and went up to Mary, the barmaid.

'Mary,' says he, 'Can you give me a loan of three euros? Paddy owes me some money and he should be in later. Here, you can have this as collateral,' taking the cheese out from under his jacket.

Mary agreed, and gave Jimmy the money, and Jimmy put the cheese down beside her before going over to the bar to order the pint he was gagging for.

A while later Paddy came into the bar and spotted Jimmy. 'Jimmy, there ya are. There's that money I owe you,' Paddy said, putting €10 down on the bar in front of his mate. Jimmy ordered another pint, and with the change he got from the barman he went back over to Mary.

'There you go Mary, there's the three euros you loaned me,' he said, putting the money down on the table and reaching out to pick up the block of cheese. But he wasn't quick enough, and Mary swiped it off the table, holding it close to her.

'Fuck off, I bought that cheese,' she said.

'No you fucking didn't,' said Jimmy. 'I gave it to you as collateral. Now give me me fucking cheese.' He lunged forward, Mary dodged him, and a row broke out.

'Give me my fucking cheese.'

'No, fuck off, I paid you for it.'

And so went the drift of the argument that, as it got louder and louder, was rapidly gaining the attention of the rest of the pub who gathered round to watch, to cheer and to offer words of encouragement to both sides of the row. The barmen came out when things looked as though they might come to blows, and somebody sent for the bouncers.

Billy, the bouncer, waded into the middle of the argument, but couldn't be heard above the shouting between Jimmy, Mary and the gathered crowd. There was no sense to be got out of any of them, so Billy decided to settle the argument once and for all by grabbing the cheese and throwing it up onto the parapet over the bar.

'Fuck the lot of you,' he said as he hurled the chunk of cheese with the skill of an Olympic shot-putter.

'Me fucking cheese, you bastard,' Jimmy said, launching himself at Billy, who had only inflamed the situation with his drastic response.

Sitting over the other side of the bar was a quiet little man, a local wino. He watched what happened from a distance, and although his brain was pickled through years of alcohol abuse, he was not one to miss out on an opportunity such as the one that had just presented itself to him.

While the kerfuffle was still going on he climbed up onto the bar, retrieved the block of cheese, and by the time everyone was thrown out of the Penthouse for fighting he had sold it, used the money to buy a bottle of VP, and was sitting on the pavement outside the pub watching the fight as it continued outside.

*   *   *

I had been living in England for a number of years when the TV licence man finally caught up with me. I had just moved into the house I live in now, and even from the front door it was easy for anyone to see that I was just moving in. But I still had the same attitude to TV licences then as I had when I lived in Ballymun. To be honest, even though I now pay this bill by direct debit, I still don't see why I should. After all, television companies are businesses like any other, so why the Hell should the general public be charged to help them with the upkeep? Why can't they use advertising and sponsorship like the independent TV companies? But anyway, back to the TV licence man at my door.

'Can I see your TV licence please?' he asked. They always ask that, even though they know full well that you don't have one, otherwise you would be on their records and they wouldn't be knocking on your door in the first place. I am sure they approach things this way just to make people feel uncomfortable from the outset.

'A what?' I replied, emphasising my Irish accent.

'A licence for your television. Do you have a television?'

'Yes, I have two,' I told him honestly.

'Are they colour or black & white?'

'Colour.'

'But you don't have a licence?' He checked again, and I frowned at him.

'I haven't got the faintest idea what you are talking about,' I said, in a performance that was Oscar-worthy.

'Have you been in the country long?' he asked. (Reeled in and landed!)

'Only a week,' I lied. And he looked at me pitifully as he explained how, in England, I needed a licence in order to watch TV legally.

'And do I have to have a licence for each telly?' I asked him. And he explained that one licence covered all televisions in my household. 'So, how much are they, and where can I buy one?'

He told me the cost and I reeled just as I would have done if I hadn't already known the extortionate cost of a licence in the first place; hence why I didn't have one. He explained that I could buy one at the post office and I assured him that I would.

'Do they not have TV licences in Ireland then?' he asked, and he probably still believes to this day that they don't.

Then he asked me if he could come in and see my two televisions, and my eyes narrowed in suspicion.

'Why would you want to do that? You already told me that one licence covers as many tellies as I own, so why do you want to come in?' He didn't answer, but shuffled off down the street; Witch-Finder General for the BBC, who are incapable of running their business without financial support from the general public.

* * *

One Ballymunner, a soldier, was chosen to stand guard over the President's body when Eamon De Valera died in 1975. We will call him John Smith, because I am sure he will not mind me using his real name. And to this day he beams with obvious pride whenever somebody mentions that sad duty. Nobody who filed past to view the President's body as it lay in state knew anything about the soldiers who stood on guard. But I am sure that every one of them felt pride in the men who stood there, not moving a muscle for hours on end. This has to be a rare occasion indeed, when thousands upon thousands of Dublin people felt pride for one Ballymunner. Nobody knew where John lived, only that he performed his duty with excellence.